How To Fight Google And Win!

By Tyronne Jacques

Listen To Us On

http://www.blogtalkradio.com/removeitnow

How To Fight Google And Win!

By Tyronne Jacques

Raegan Publishing

The artwork for the cover was provided by Ronelle Collins of Two Things Graphic Design, all photos used were acquired as stock photos.

Visit the author's website www.removeslander.com

For booking information or interviews please send your request to tyronnejacques@gmail.com

Published by Raegan Publishing, LLC

Raegan Publishing
2159 Rapatel Street
Mandeville La 70448

Library of congress control number
Printed in the United States of America

ISBN: 978-0-615-39667-5

First Edition: August 2010

Special Thanks

This book wouldn't be possible without the support and sacrifice of a few special people.

To my mom Catherine Jacques Davis – Thank you for giving birth to me twice in one lifetime. When I didn't feel going forward in life, you pushed me forward.

To Peach (Chantrell Jacques), Irvin Davis, Raymond Jacques, Walter Jacques, Earl Weaver Jr., and Mary Jacques (Grand mom), the sacrifices you made for me will never be forgotten. Thank you!

To my children - who inspire me every day to be a better father, I did this for you.
To my oldest daughter Aymani Jacques, I love you and I accept your challenge.

To Sherman Campbell, Larry Johnson, and Ronald Gullage you remain closer than a brother in my heart.

To my siblings – I challenge you to accomplish your dreams, as I continue to chase mine.

To Ronelle Collins – Thank you for loving me through it all, unquestionable Love. Thank you for all of your support and believing that we can accomplish anything.

To my Dad, I need you now more than ever!

P.S – I will need all of you again for my next project, so don't go anywhere.

"Speak To The Air."

TABLE OF CONTENTS

Let's Get Ready To Rumble!

INTRODUCTION

I Understand

I know how it feels to have humiliating information on the first page of Google. I know how it feels to have an old incident haunt you every time someone searches your name in Google. The humiliation derived from having a part of your life posted unfairly online can lead to enormous aggravation and depression.

The worst part of an online attack is that Internet searchers tend to accept the first page search results as factual.

Whatever content that manages to land on the first page of your search results can cause a tremendous amount of grief, and loss of revenue for your business. The fact that you're even reading this book tells me that you are concerned about your online reputation or the reputation of your business.

In 2007 I experienced my own online attack which was launched by one of my competitors. As long as I was charging my clients $2500 to remove just one negative link from the first page of Google, no one had a problem with me. The gates of hell opened up at the exact moment I created my own niche, and lowered my prices to res more affordable for my clients.

Few things are worse than coming under attack from one of your competitors for simply trying to make a living. Then to add insult to injury, the guy sends me an e-mail from the *Contact Us* page on my own website informing us that he was anonymously doing it.

I was crushed!

The reason it hurt so much was because I would have never even thought about posting insidious content about one of my competitors. I tried to reach out to everyone in the business. Here is one of the main points that I want you to retain from this book.

The Internet has created a forum whereas any anonymous person can post numerous defamatory comments and the search engines will index it.

The only advantage I had over you is I knew what to do the moment the lies were indexed by Google. Having said that, it was still very painful to review the content posted about my business, especially since all of my customers were extremely happy with our services.

I have put my heart, soul, and countless hours into my business, which fully explained my next set of emotions: anger! The rage that came over me was enough motivation to launch a counterattack like the world has not seen since storming the Beaches at Normandy.

I wanted revenge!

There are some in battles in life that are better fought indirectly rather than head on, and Internet slander is one of them. So once I cooled off and took the advice from one of my most trusted colleagues, I decided that the best approach to my online attack falls in line with the advice I give my clients every day.

Focus on building a wall around your brand, and it will protect you from all harm and online defamation.

One of my challenges was I became so busy lecturing, writing, and advising clients that I totally forgot to man my own fort. I was so busy protecting the online reputation of major corporations that I totally forgot to protect my own, which left us exposed.

When I said at the beginning of this chapter that I totally understand you, I mean I totally understand you. You never anticipate that something as simple as a blog post calling you or your business a scam was going to cause such a hurricane in your life.

You never anticipate that your five-year relationship would end on such a sour note that it would result in your ex posting horrible comments and private pictures of you all over the Internet. Nor did you ever image that your DUI arrest would not only make the crime section of the local newspaper but also land on the first page of Google directly under your name.

Who would have figured?

Like you, I was busy running my business, and enjoying my life. I never had the time to sit down and calculate an attack on someone else, nor did I want to. And even I have to admit that I had developed the same false sense of security of a sovereign nation, only to have that security stripped away with one online terrorist attack. It basically left me asking myself over and over again, what did I do this guy to deserve this?

The reality is many of the attacks against people like you are senseless and unwarranted. They can happen as randomly as an inner city drive by, or as calculated as a political smear campaign.

An online attack is not only an attack on your reputation; it is also an attack on your credibility. Internet slander can take you from a position of notoriety, to obscurity within 60 days. From a thriving prosperous corporation, to a dwindling struggling entity all before Thanksgiving arrives.

Is it fair? No.

Does it happen every day? Yes

Every day the reputation of a business or the reputation of a teen comes under attack in the form of a slanderous website. Sometimes posted on blogs or even private forums, the damage is almost instant once posted.

Before you become too exasperated with the Internet please allow me to defend it in this one statement, the Internet is being totally misused for the purpose of slander.

Bob Kahn and Vint Cerf vision of the Internet in 1972 basically involved the idea of a Transmission Control Protocol (TCP) that moves data on the modern version of our Internet.

Even in all of their brilliance I am sure that they could have never imagined that their shared invention would be used as an electronic toilet.

This is the only reason that I can come to the defense of the Internet because as a standalone item, it is merely a tool. Like any tool used incorrectly it does possess the potential to cause a great deal of harm.

The Internet was used as a tool to attack you. Something that is very pure in its functionality has been corrupted in a way that has led to the distortion of your online reputation.

So when I said earlier that I totally understand how you feel right now, I am speaking from firsthand experience. Every emotion your feeling right now, I have already experienced.

The reason my attack was so embarrassing was due to the fact that I am in the field of Reputation Management.

18

The fact that I was attacked online is sort of like the barber who really needs a haircut or a dentist who really need braces, it just shouldn't happen.

At this point I hope it gives you some comfort in knowing that I experienced the same type of attack you experienced, but this is where you will really receive some concrete assurance. I have either battled or witnessed every type of online attack.

Everything from attacks in blogs, forums, complaint sites, fake online articles, impersonated profiles, social media, online stalking, and created domains, I have seen it all. Not only have I seen it all, but I have also declared war on each of the attacks that I've just mentioned. My intent in that statement is not merely pretentious; just consider it more as the announcement of my fight record as an experienced boxer.

The benefit to you is I have learned something from each of my battles, and many of those lessons I am now passing on to you.

CHAPTER 1

The Good News

ℰℐℭℬ

I do not think there is any other quality so essential to success of any kind as the quality of perseverance. It overcomes almost everything.

ℰℐℭℬ

Here is the good news:

- You are not alone
- You are not the only one that this is happening to
- You can overcome this challenge
- You can recover your online reputation
- You can stop the loss of revenue as a result of online defamation
- You have a right to remove negative items from the 1st page of search engines.

The ultimate good news is that you have the right to present a more positive image of your life and your business. My goal is to empower you with real information on how to build a fence around your first page search results.

On the surface your counterattack is really simple, even if the task is daunting. Our goal is to remove your negative item from the first page of search engines as well as prevent those items from returning.

The only reason we are even having this conversation is because the item that is causing you so much aggravation is now located somewhere near the top of your search results. If this item was on page 5 then chances are it would not even be worth mentioning, but location is indeed everything when it comes to business.

The location of this ugly link is in a place where everyone can see it, which is totally unacceptable.

If your attack came in the form of an ex-girlfriend who posted comments in a blog calling you a "Cheating Dog," warning that "all women should beware of this guy," then it would make it extremely difficult to form new relationships without this hovering dark cloud.

If your attack came in the form of a former employee who decided to post your sensitive trade secrets online, then it could destroy your competitive edge.

Or imagine if you will, having your 15- year-old daughter branded as a slut by a group of rival cheerleaders, as they post her picture on fake MySpace accounts.

I have just given you a brief overview of the anatomy of an online attack. From this point forward we will begin to examine many types of strategies to deal with all of the attacks that I have just presented, but the before mentioned was not the purpose of this chapter.

The purpose of this chapter was to let you know that I know how it feels to be you. I am very familiar with the fear of my new client (that I having been pursuing for six months) discovering what has been posted about my business online. I know how it feels to avoid public gatherings because your paranoia is telling you that everyone is talking about "that link" located on the first page of your search results.

Now that you understand that I know what this moment feels like for you, we can now begin the process of repairing it. So how do we fix it?

We will fix this situation with relentless diligence, proven strategies, and aggressive persistence. As deliberate as your attacker was in defaming you, we will be even more preemptive in our response. The only difference is we will not respond directly to our attacker, but all of our efforts will employ the laws of strategic misdirection.

As we begin to train for your heavy weight bout against your online attacker, all I ask is that you take just a little time to absorb the theory embedded within this book.

Search engines like Google are constantly changing their approach to how they will rank websites, and likewise your strategy will have to adjust overtime.

Despite the shift in Google's ranking systems there is one thing that will remain the same, Google loves relevant content.

With this basic principle in mind, my goal is to teach you how to work within Google's system to move a negative site off the first page. To accomplish this goal I must make you fluent in SEO = Search Engine Optimization Strategies.

SEO is the only way to move a site off the first page of Google. Search Engine Optimization is the process of getting websites to rank high in Google and remain relevant to the assigned keyword.

My goal is to provide this information in very simple, and easy to follow format that will allow you to adjust whenever Google makes adjustments.

As I mentioned earlier, our goal is not simply to remove the negative item, but to make sure that a damaging website never lands on your 1st page again.

You will become your own Department of Homeland Security, as you defend your name and your brand from online terrorists.

As part of your training camp we have also included our *"How to Fight Google and Win"* lectures, which will walk you through the strategy step by step. We are fully aware that no strategy is permanent therefore we offer regular updates on our website www.removeslander.com

To receive free access to the lectures, send an email to tj@removeitnow.com with the ISBN number and we will send you an e-mail with the link and password information.

Finally, please keep in mind that some of these strategies will have an immediate impact on your first page search results but others will take days or even weeks to settle in. Once they settle in, these techniques will begin the process of building that fence around your 1st page search results.

Now lace up your sneakers, start your warm up stretches, and let's get ready to work.

CHAPTER 2

The Anatomy of the Attack

ℰℭ

The opportunity of a lifetime must be seized within the lifetime of the opportunity.

ℰℭ

Your name is your brand.

I know that may sound like an obvious statement, but as the Internet continues to emerge as the marketplace of choice you will have to become more aggressive in the defense of your brand.

Long before Google, if a customer had an issue with you or your business they would simply storm into your location and demand to speak with the manager.

Now they storm onto Google and trash the reputation of your business with the use of Consumer Complaint Sites.

In no way am I discrediting all consumer complaints as shallow, but the popularity of sites like Rip-Off Report and Complaints.com has become a hub for insidious content.

To make matters worse search engines like Google take no responsibility for the content posted by 3rd parties; however Google is also financing and legitimizing these sites with their Google AdSense campaigns.

So now you have two separate parties benefiting from one lie posted about you or your business. To paint an even clearer picture for you, we will now examine what I call the "Slander for Cash Scheme."

Slander for Cash Scheme

1. A customer enters your mechanic shop interested in getting a wheel alignment on their 2004 Honda Civic. After you check their car you discover that they also need four new tires and back rotors. You give the customer the price for the wheel alignment but also inform them that they need four new tires and two back rotors or the problem will persist. The customer determines that they will only pay for

the wheel alignment and nothing more. After two months has passed, the wheel alignment is now offset again because of the poor quality of the tires. The same customer storms into your location demanding a refund, at that point you pull your notes from the transaction and politely inform them of your recommendations at the time of their last service visit. The customer becomes angry because you refused to give them a refund or re-align the car for free.

2. Customer then in turn contacts the local Better Business Bureau and files a complaint claiming that your business is a scam. In addition to the complaint with the local BBB the customer also posts a one paragraph entry on Rip-Off Report calling you a scam artist, and your business a scam. In their posting on the complaint site the customer makes no mention that you advised them that they would need four new tires, and new rotors. Now you are noticing a decline in your clientele, and the national roadside companies are no longer sending you emergency calls. Despite the fact you have been in business for more than 15 years and have built an impressive reputation in your town, this one online post is now eroding your business.

You have no idea why you are losing sales and have dropped down to a few loyal customers. Then one day your 16-year-old daughter informs you that there is a negative article about you in Google. You heart rate increases as you type your name into the Google search box, and there it is in bold at the top of the page "ABC Auto Is a Scam."

3. You try to repost what happened in an attempt to prove that your business is not a scam. You even try to contact the complaint site and ask them to take the page down, but cannot get anyone to reply to your e-mails. As you look closer at the negative post you notice that a few people have added anonymous comments also calling your business a scam.

   Your gut tells you that the other posts are from the same guy because they were posted only minutes apart, but nevertheless all of the posts are listed under your name.

   You also notice that several ads for Reputation Management companies are along the sides of the complaint site, advertising that they can remove negative sites like the one you're on. Then to add insult to injury you receive an email from the host of the site six weeks later saying that they are willing to remove the link for a fee of $3500. You contact your attorney in an attempt to sue the site for slander only to be informed that they are protected under freedom of speech laws.

Here is another example for you to consider:

You work at a high school in which one of your fellow teachers has been accused of inappropriate behavior with a student.

On the surface this incident has nothing to do with you with the exception that you confiscated a note that was being passed around by other students in which they described the details of the teacher / Student relationship.

So eventually the relationship between the student and the teacher comes to a climatic end with the story getting blasted all over the news.

The teacher gets arrested and faces a long list of charges with Statutory Rape being the most serious one on the list. Now it's time for the trial, and being that this event took place in Small Town America which only has one newspaper and one local news network, the coverage of the event is intense.

You're still thanking your lucky stars that this event has nothing to do with you until one day you get served to appear in court as a material witness.

It seems that the word has gotten out that you knew of the event prior to the story breaking and failed to report it to the authorities. So now not only do you have to testify, but you have just been toss into the middle of a hell hole that you didn't create.

It's now the day of the trial and you have just provided testimony that you were, in fact, aware of the events due to the note that you confiscated from the students. Despite the fact that you're not the one on trial, you are still getting tried in the court of public opinion for your failure to report the relationship between the teacher and the student.

Unbeknownst to you, as you were giving your testimony a reporter from the local newspaper was transcribing your every word as a part of the coverage of the trial. The next day the headline reads "High School Molestation – Not the Musical."

You never really gave the newspaper article any thought because your role in the entire trial was only as a witness, not the accused.

Until one month later when your brother calls you to inform you that if someone conducts a search for your name in Google, the item at the very tops says "High School Molestation – Not the Musical."

How could this happen you ask? It happened because the newspaper reporter simply included your name in the story, and now when your name is searched the article will appears at the top of your search results.

I wanted to tell this story because it happened exactly as I described it. I am sure you can see how devastating this could be to someone who was simply complying with the orders of the court but had nothing to do with the event. Many of times your name can get connected to a negative event by association, which at first glance would cause Internet searchers to form the wrong opinion of you.

When President Bill Clinton signed into law Section 230 of the Communications Decency Act in 1996, I am sure that he had no idea that it would be used in such a horrific manner.

Now let us examine how this attack was able to land on the first page of Google. For Google to find this item the customer in our first example had to post the complaint using the name of the company in either the title or the tags.

Simply placing the name of the business in the tags (list of keywords) will not guarantee that this item will land on the first page, but placing the name of the business in the title of the attack site is a definite.

In the second example the name of the teacher was simply mentioned in a newspaper article.

Once search engines conduct their crawls (or updates) this article will get indexed because it is considered to be relevant content. Search engines are in love with content relevant to a selected keyword.

In the example of the teacher, this wasn't a negative attack from an online terrorist, but rather an inclusion due to relevance.

> *Every day thousands of false allegations are posted online by customers who unfairly accuse legitimate businesses of operating as scams.*

The Only Cure

I spend most of my time studying SEO (Search Engine Optimization) more than anything else despite the fact all of my credentials say Reputation Management Expert. The reason is simple, the more I learn about SEO, the more effective I will be at Online Reputation Management.

As The Book of Genesis says Cush begat Nimrod, so does Search Engine Optimization begat Reputation Management. You will not accomplish movement on the first page of Google unless you absorb the basics of SEO. Believe me when I say this, it's not that hard.

What Actually Happened To You

I have created an algebraic expression designed to help you understand how this online attack was able to land on the first page of your search results. It wasn't an accident; someone used your name or the name of your business in sequential detail in order to land their attack perfectly at the top of your search results.

Here is the equation:

$$T + N(C) = L$$

For clarity please allow me to explain it this way. The **T**itle that included your **N**ame, factored by the amount of **C**ompetition for your name on the first page, will determine the **L**ocation of your negative content.

Title + Name * Competition = Location

The reason a negative link was able to rank so high within your search results is due to the lack of competition for your Keyword. In your case the keyword used to attack you, was your name or business name.

This attack formula is not likely to have the same amount of success if your name or business name was Coca-Cola because of the (C) variable.

Unlike your name, their exist a ton of sites all competing to land on the first page under the keyword Coca-Cola, so there is little probability of an attack site landing there.

Once Google or any search engine crawls the Internet seeking new and updated content, they normally find websites that are appropriately tagged. Google indexing process is based on the results discovered by what they refer to as Spiders.

Think of spiders as actual spiders that searched the Internet, and found a negative website that happen to have your name embedded.

Once collected, the next thing the spider will do is make suggestions about where to place the negative site.

Unfortunately, the spider placed the slanderous site directly on the first page of your search results.

The business owner of ABC Auto discovered his insidious site on the first page of Google, directly under his name. Upon discovering it his first reaction was to contact the website and ask them to take it down because it contained information was totally false. The business owner very quickly realized that at this exact moment in time there isn't a branch of government committed to protecting consumers from online defamation.

If you have been attacked in a similar fashion as described at the beginning of this chapter then you will have to go at it alone to protect and clear your name.

If you plan to take on your attack link on your own then I need you to resist the urge to skip forward to the strategies sections of this book without getting the theory of these first few chapters.

> *In fact the Internet is the new Wild-Wild West with no Wyatt Earp, no James Ernest, or Lone Ranger to protect you.*

It is in the theory that I will teach you how to remove a negative site even if Google rearranges their criteria for ranking websites.

It is very important that you understand what you're up against, and why the attack was able to go public without any fear of a Defamation of Character lawsuit.

CHAPTER 3

Why Google Could Care Less

ဆာ၀၃

In the confrontation between the stream and the rock, the stream always wins- not through strength but by perseverance.

ဆာ၀၃

The reason why Google could care less is that Google cannot be sued for slander in a United States Court of Law.

That's right; you cannot sue Google for slander even if every word on the attack website calling your daughter a slut is a complete lie. Google can care less because Congress gave them total immunity, and a license to participate in the destruction of the online reputation of your child.

Google operates without fear of consequence, without risk off loss associated with the online content on the site, and without concern or compassion for the lives being harmed by their search engine results.

Why Can't I Sue Google for Slander?

The above question can be categorized as one of those "if I only had a dime for every time I was asked" questions. As Google has grown in size and power on the Internet so have the many misuses of its search engine capabilities.

Here is the major problem with a search engine like Google. The only content that they will monitor is child porn sites, and terrorist hubs. Other than the before mentioned sites, everything else is allowed without question. Another problem many people are experiencing with Google is that the site has become sort of an unregulated verification service.

Unregulated in the sense that any anonymous person can publish just about anything (regardless if it is true or not) and Google will index it.

Unlike real third-party reporting agencies or background verification services, which are regulated by FCRA and can be held libel, search engines are not required to fact check any of their content.

I am sure you can see how this could be very problematic r for you or the reputation of your business.

If you are a business owner of a coffee shop, and some guy decides to go on a crazed posting blitz on Google because you screwed up his latte', then the reputation of your business can take a very serious hit.

So before you run off and pay some lawyer guy hundreds or even thousands of dollars please allow me to say this again, you can't sue Google.

You simply can't do it, no matter how false or erroneous the content, you cannot sue Google.

Blame it on Bill Clinton

The Great Bill Clinton may have presided over the most powerful US Economy since WWII, but the signing of The Communications Decency Act of 1996 (*CDA*) could be one of the worst forms of legislation ever signed into Law.

Here is why this could be one of the worst Acts ever: Section 230!

Section 230 basically says that you cannot sue a site like Google for any content posted by a 3rd party.

This slimy little section provides total immunity for service providers (like Google), out of fear that holding them libel would create censorship and violate freedom of speech in online forums and content.

Here is how that section of the bill reads:

(C) **Protection for "Good Samaritan" blocking and screening of offensive material**

(1) **Treatment of publisher or speaker** - No provider or user of an interactive computer service shall be treated as the publisher or speaker of any information provided by another information content provider.

(2) **Civil liability** - No provider or user of an interactive computer service shall be held liable on account of—

(A) any action voluntarily taken in good faith to restrict access to or availability of material that the provider or user considers to be obscene, lewd, lascivious, filthy, excessively violent, harassing, or otherwise objectionable, whether or not such material is constitutionally protected; or

(B) Any action taken to enable or make available to information content providers or others the technical means to restrict access to material described in paragraph.

I hate to be the bearer of bad news for those of you who were expecting to have your day in court in the epic battle of You versus Google, it will never happen.

This section of the Act has come under criticism for unleashing the power of the Internet in the worst possible way, which breeds online slander.

Gregory Dickerson's entry into the Harvard Journal of Law and Public Policy has not only been the best description of the legal issues created by Section 230, but also provides us with pathway to correct this flawed piece of legislation.

"Almost all courts to interpret Section 230 of the Communications Decency Act have construed its ambiguously worded immunity provision broadly, shielding Internet intermediaries from tort liability so long as they are not the literal authors of offensive content. Although this broad interpretation affects the basic goals of the statute, it ignores several serious textual difficulties and mistakenly extends protection too far by immunizing even direct participants in tortuous conduct."

> **At some point Congress will have to reconsider restoring service provider's liability in some cases, which will do far more to reestablish the integrity of online content.**

"This analysis, which examines the text and history of Section 230

in light of two strains of pre-Internet vicarious liability defamation doctrine, concludes that the immunity provision of Section 230, though broad, was not intended to abrogate entirely traditional common law notions of vicarious liability. Some bases of vicarious liability remain, and their continuing validity both explains the textual puzzles courts have faced in applying Section 230 and undergirds the push by a small minority of courts to narrow the section's immunity provision."

The highlight of this entire section states that the posters are still liable although, their identities are protected from disclosure by First Amendment theories regarding anonymous speech, which explains why are online attacks are anonymous.

Guilty as Charged!

Some websites like Rip-Off Report and Complaints Board have exploited and corrupted Section 230 to profit from consumer complaints.

Google has basically crawled in bed with slanderous sites like Rip-Off Report that claim to provide a public forum. Google rewards complaint sites by placing their AdWords (Pay per Click Ads) on every false claim submitted to the Rip-Off Report

And if that wasn't slimy enough, the Rip-Off Report will allow a false claim to be published about a business on their website and then contact that company with an offer to remove the claim for a small fee off $3500 to $10,000.

I cannot understand why Google has allowed itself to become a repository for malicious graffiti.

I have reviewed their standards and requirements for ranking a website many of times and I cannot understand why they would allow themselves to be affiliated with a site like Rip-Off Report.

Here are just a few of the allegations that have been directed at this one site.

- The site creates complaints against legitimate small business and corporations, and then contacts the company to offer their Corporate Advocacy Program.

- Even if the person mentioned in the Rip-Off Report contacts the site with proof that the allegations are false, the ROR will not remove the complaint.

- Business owners who reply to the complaints posted about their business are horrified to discover that ROR has listed their comments as a new complaint.

Despite Google's ongoing relationship Rip-Off Report, Yahoo and Bing should receive a hand clap of praise for completely banning the site from their search engine results.

Hungry for Content

Another reason Google could care less about the attack against you or your business is because Internet slander equates to content and search engines are addicted to content, any type of content.

Content will always mean traffic, and traffic to a search engine will always produce cash, even if it's generated by negative content.

Search engines have discovered that if they collect everything published onto the Internet then someone will eventually read it, even if there is only one person featured in the story.

Their ultimate goal is to keep searchers glued to their site, which allows them to turn to the advertisers and say "over 100 million searches were conducted on our site last month."

It is this idea of *Content is King* that has caused search engines to participate in the destruction of thousands of online reputations around the world. Some would argue that one post claiming that a business is operating as a scam, is not enough to demand a total overhaul of Section 230 but those comments are always made by someone who has yet to be called a scam in an online forum.

This belief that consumers no longer accept online content as authentic is hollow and only proves that the person making the comment is either a lawyer for Google, or totally detached from the real world.

The reality is that the items listed on the first page of search results will not only be considered factual but will affect purchasing decisions.

Facebook, Twitter and Craigslist

Facebook, Twitter, and Craigslist all have benefited from this enormous loop hole that has allowed them to escape any and all liability associated with online content posted by a third party.

Craigslist has recently come under fire for its association with prostitution, the sale of stolen goods, and child trafficking associated with prostitution.

Craigslist has repeatedly taunted its critics because of its immunity status and has demonstrated time and time again that not even local law enforcement can penetrate their wall of immunity.

Despite claiming to take no responsibility for the content posted by its members, Craigslist is fully aware that posters are using the site to sell and solicit sex.

While conducting research for this book I came across various bloggers who were complaining about how

Craigslist repeatedly allowed ads for their businesses to get flagged, while allowing a sexual solicitation ad from an 18-year-old girl in Jackson, Mississippi to remain for 30 consecutive days.

Facebook has also done its part in abusing Section 230 by allowing the site to become the forum of choice for cyber-bully attacks.

Back when I was in high school if you were bullied it pretty much was an in school incident, but now bullying has a far more reaching impact.

If you are a current victim of bullying, chances are the fist-fighting is taking place over a social networking site like Twitter or Facebook.

When I was bullied in high school, I only had to worry about some guy taking my lunch money. But if I were bullied today, then there is a chance I could have my pictures, and a ton of derogatory comments posted all over the web.

Both Facebook and Craigslist have made claims that it is impossible to monitor or censor the content posted by their members because of the sheer number of posts per day. What I have found interesting about this claim is that they have the extraordinary ability to block unauthorized ads in a very precise fashion.

Spam, duplicate content, and multi-level marketing ads are all rooted out by Facebook instantly the moment the items are posted which leaves very little excuse for allowing defamatory content.

Facebook claims that it was unaware of case of 15-year-old Phoebe Prince, who committed suicide as a result of cyber-bullying.

PleaseRobMe.com has become locked in battle with Twitter for exposing the vulnerability of Tweeters who Tweet their every move. PleaseRobMe.com seems to suggest that your home could get burglarized as a result of your tweets which indirectly broadcasted that no one was home.

The site makes the same claim as Twitter which stands behind their unified response to criticism; once the items are posted it then becomes public information.

> *Perhaps the greatest challenge to Section 230 will not come from the prostitution rings embedded in Craigslist or by the prison yard atmosphere created by Facebook, but from a prank site called PleaseRobMe.com.*

There has yet to be any reported incidents of homes that have been burglarized due to the information posted on PleaseRobMe.com, but the site has definitely exposed the problem with granting an entity total immunity from liability.

Sites like Google, Twitter, PleaseRobMe, Facebook and Craigslist all are symptoms of a greater illness, Section 230 of The Communication Decency Act of 1996. At some point Congress will have to revisit this issue of allowing service providers to simply hide behind Section 230.

All throughout history our constitution has protected freedom of speech, while simultaneously protecting individuals and corporations from defamation and slander. The same laws that have applied to print media and traditional journalism should apply to Internet service providers.

The laws that regulate what is considered defamation of character has created a platform whereas all facts are checked for accuracy and truth prior to the content being reported or published.

This system has ensured the integrity of our press, and if applied to online media will only improve the quality of online sources.

Until Congress takes on the issues of the lawlessness that exist within sites like Google, Facebook, and

Craigslist, you will have to take the necessary steps to protect yourself. Welcome to the Wild-Wild West.

CHAPTER 4

Google's Dominance of the UK

❧❧

Most of the important things in the world have been accomplished by people who have kept on trying when there seemed to be no help at all.

❧❧

The End of Net Neutrality

How big is too big? Google may very well find itself on the same side of this question as Standard Oil, Microsoft, and Ma Bell *The American Bell Telephone Company.* Google has not only dominated the American market in both online search and advertising but has also conducted a clean sweep of the UK Markets as well.

The major issue with Google's dominance has yet to be realized by many consumers because they have still maintained fairly high approval ratings, but Microsoft would beg to differ.

The competitors of Google are up in arms over the issue of Net Neutrality. Google's invasion of the UK is the equivalent of the British musicians invasion of the US in the 1960s; everyone thought it was great with the exception of the Blues Singers.

Similar to their rise to power in United States, Google emerged as the dominant player in the UK without any major advertisement or fanfare.

The UK Invasion

Internet Searchers in the UK woke up one morning and Google was everywhere, over 80% of the searches were conducted on this one site.

Don't get me wrong I am not against the success of Google. Many people throughout history have shared my same concerns whenever they were confronted with a real-life Monopoly. In my lifetime I thought I would never see the day when a company such as Microsoft would whine and cry foul over the success of Google.

It's amazing how the tables have turned from the mid-90s when Google was one of the leading cheerleaders in the antitrust battle against Microsoft; now Google is Goliath.

What happened to the UK based company Foundem.com can happen to any company that stands directly in the way of Google's ambitions.

There is a distinct difference between using your strength as a corporation to advance your company, and using your strength to prevent another corporation from existing within your market.

Google has used its strength to basically bury Foundem.com only because they occupied an area that became attractive to Google; shopping searches.

Looks like Standard Oil, Smells like Standard Old

At the core of all monopolies is the need to dominate their market, partnered with their desire to eliminate the competition. Standard Oil made it virtually impossible for anyone to coexist with them at the height of their power.

Even supporters of an extreme doctrine of free enterprise would still have to side with the position of the government in cases such as Ma Bell and Standard Oil because the consumers will ultimately suffer.

For anyone who doubts that this is an issue then all they have to do is examine one of Google's most successful products, AdWords. Google's AdWords has come under fire for what is known as Click Fraud.

Google AdWords is a pay per click system that allows advertisers to only pay once a customer clicks one of their ads. At the same time Google's AdSense allows affiliate marketers to receive commissions for driving traffic to paid advertisements which is also determined by clicks.

Advertisers in the UK and the United States are now coming to realization that many of the clicks they were charged for were actually made by affiliates who received commissions resulting from clicks. Google is the beneficiary of billions of dollars from advertisers in the UK and the United States.

Google is also the beneficiary of revenues lost by advertisers as the result of Click Fraud.

Of course Google claims that they have placed preventative measures in place that protect advertisers from losses related to click fraud, but more and more claims are starting to surface.

The advertisers have to basically eat the loss because of the sheer number of searches that Google has, but it still equates to theft.

Click fraud is just one of the examples of what can happen when a corporation like Google is allowed to regulate itself.

Many consumers are totally unaware of how controlled their search results really are but competitors of Google are very familiar with its lock on search results.

Once you type a keyword or phrase into the Google search bar, they will determine what search results appear.

Buried Alive

This is the major issue and complaint of UK companies like Foundem.com who found themselves in the crosshairs of the Google Sniper. Google launched its Universal Search in 2007 which targeted Maps, Shopping, Books, Video, and News. "The ultimate goal of Universal Search is to break down the silos of information that exist on the web and provide the very best answer every time a user enters a query," explained Google vice president Marissa Mayer. "The best answer will appear in a single set of blended search results."

Of course you can see why Google would suppress any other product except their own within the results. It almost seems naïve that we would think that Google would include any other product above their own products; after all there are benefits to having a conflict of interest.

But the issue before us now is Google controls more than 70% of the market share. Once a company has reached more than 70% of the market share they are now subject to antitrust regulations. Google was able to penetrate the UK markets fairly easy because it was also able to suppress all of its competitors on page 10, 11, and 12 of its search results.

John Battelle noted in 2008 that "Google is becoming more and more of a media company in the traditional sense in that it is driving traffic to properties it already owns."

"And whether or not it does so with transparency, and whether or not we believe that it truly is the best place to end up -- on their maps as opposed to MapQuest or whatever -- the truth is that the interface that's being created, this sort of one-box, universal blended interface that's starting to appear on Google is forcing a renegotiation of the relationship between content owners and Google."

The European Commission, Europe's highest antitrust authority, is currently looking into "some allegations of anticompetitive conduct in relation to search," says Joaquin Almunia, Vice-Pres of the European commission in charge of competition policy. It appears that Almunia is wrestling with whether Google is blocking access to their competitors and if searchers find these competitors by using other means?

All Mr. Almunia has to do is examine the carnage of companies that have succumbed to the wrath of Google.

A consumer watchdog recently hand-delivered a very damaging report to U.S. Justice Department and European Commission antitrust officials on the practices of Google titled - "Traffic Report: How Google is Squeezing out Competitors and Muscling Into New Markets."

According to John M. Simpson -The study of Internet traffic data for more than 100 popular websites since 2007 revealed Google's dramatic gains.

In the most comprehensive study of its kind to date, Inside Google obtained three years of Internet traffic data from the respected web metrics firm Experian Hitwise. The data allowed an analysis of Google's business practices and performance that is unprecedented in scope.

The data shows that Google has established a Microsoft-like monopoly in some key areas of the web. In video, Google has nearly doubled its market share to almost 80%.

That is the legal definition of a monopoly, according to the federal courts, which have held that a firm achieves "monopoly power" when it gains between 70% and 80% of a market, the report noted.

Below I have included the Executive Summary of the report "How Google is Squeezing out Competitors and Muscling Into New Markets" for your review.

Executive Summary

Google has been muscling into new web markets and greatly expanding its dominance of other web commerce sectors since 2007, when the web search giant adopted a controversial new business practice aimed at steering Internet searchers to its own services.

Google's dramatic gains are revealed by an analysis of internet traffic data for more than 100 popular websites. Once upon a time, these sites primarily benefited from Google.

Now, they must also compete with it. In the most comprehensive study of its kind to date, INSIDE GOOGLE obtained three years of traffic data from the respected web metrics firm Experian Hitwise, allowing an analysis of Google's business practices and performance that is unprecedented in scope.

The data shows that Google has established a Microsoft-like monopoly in some key areas of the web. In video, Google has nearly doubled its market share to almost 80%. That is the legal definition of a monopoly, according to the federal courts, which have held that a firm achieves "monopoly power" when it gains between 70% and 80% of a market.

The report examines whether Google has erected "barriers to entry" in markets such as video by manipulating its search results so that users are directed primarily or exclusively toward Google's own services, such as YouTube.

Google's dominance in video and its huge gains in other markets such as local search and comparison shopping correlates with these increasing efforts by Google to promote its own services within search results.

 This practice, which amounts to a new business model, appears to be an abandonment of Google's pledge to provide neutral search capability.

The most striking example of how this practice enables Google to muscle its way into new markets is the lucrative market for local search.

Google now inserts results from Google Maps into the first page of results from most Google searches, driving enormous traffic toward Google Maps and away from competitors. Google now has more than half the market for local search.

The ultimate significance of these developments is that they spell a rapid decline in choice for consumers. Increasingly, consumers who use Google are placing themselves in a sort of virtual gated community, or what was once known as "a company town." You can go anywhere you like, as long as you use the company's roads. And you can buy anything you like, as long as you shop at the company's stores."

Whether its click fraud or the suppression of inferior competitors in search results; Google has definitely proven its intentions of becoming the sole Internet search option. Some would even argue how can we blame them for being successful?

My answer to this question points to historical examples of companies that totally owned their industry. Corporation can never be left to their own devices; consumer protection is the reason for my concern.

With so much of our daily lives connected to the Internet my concern is that Google will begin to funnel every search to one of its own properties. It is true that internet searchers have given Google its power because without the searchers a need for Google wouldn't exist. The truth of the matter is Google provides a service to those who are seeking information; the problem comes in when Google begins to control the information that is visible.

Let Them Eat Cake

Marissa Meyer of Google once said "With Universal Search, we're attempting to break down the walls that traditionally separated our various search properties and integrate the vast amounts of information available into one simple set of search results," she writes. "We want to help you find the very best answer, even if you don't know where to look."

I ask that you look beyond the arrogance within her statement to find the meaning of what she is really saying, please allow me to translate.

"Being that you don't know the answer to your question, we will in turn provide you with a list of answers that we want you to have."

Many Internet searchers may not have an issue with Google controlling all of their information. For some this may take the burden of having to screen the information they're receiving, and that's okay. However, there is something potentially dangerous about allowing one single source to provide you with all of your information. Opponents of *Communism* may feel that one entity should never possess that much power.

There was a clear example of this threat in the 2008 Presidential Election in which candidates received questions from audience members via YouTube.

During the Presidential Debate viewers were able to submit their questions via YouTube Videos and the presidential candidates would oblige them with an answer.

At first I thought to myself "wow this is a great way to hear the voice of the people," and then it dawned on me that the questions were being submitted with the use of Google.

According to Tech Crunch "For the second quarter of 2010, Google spent $1.34 million in lobbying efforts, up 41 percent from the same quarter last year.

The number is on par with the amount Google spent on government relations in the first quarter this year, in which the search giant paid $1.38 million to influence lawmakers and regulators."

Google says that the reason it increased its spending on government lobbyists was to inform lawmakers on all of the intricate details of their industry.

The one thing that we know for sure about lobbyists and Washington DC is whoever spends the most, will receive the most.

With so many lobbyists roaming the halls of Washington this may also explain why Google has been allowed to flex its muscles without any fear of government antitrust regulations.

As MapQuest has fallen to the bottom of their industry so too will other corporations once Google has identified their niche as the next stop on the march to global dominance.

Nice Try China

To the United Kingdom, I'm sorry to inform you that you are now infected with the same disease that has crippled the Internet in the United States.

As China battled Google over the content of its search results, they were left with no other choice but to create their own state-run search engine. Unlike the UK, China will still have the luxury of controlling its own media.

The UK & United States will have to find some way of corralling Google back into the stalls of manageable regulations that allows for fair competition.

It is not a question of whether or not Google is a monopoly; the only question is how will the government break it up?

CHAPTER 5

What We Can Learn From Liskula Cohen versus Google?

ॐ

Patience and perseverance have a magical effect before which difficulties disappear and obstacles vanish

ॐ

Liskula Cohen may have exposed a chink in the armor of Google with her victory in the Manhattan Supreme Court in 2009. Toronto-native Liskula Cohen sought to unmask the writer who maligned her on the "Skanks in NYC" blog so that she could sue for defamation.

Google fought every attempt to disclose the name of the blogger arguing that the blogger's identity was protected under section 230 of the Communication Decency Act, but Judge Joan Madden firmly disagreed with Google's argument.

In her decision, Judge Joan Madden wrote that, "the thrust of the blog is that [Cohen] is a sexually promiscuous woman," and Cohen is therefore entitled to file a defamation lawsuit.

The ruling not only hand-delivered Cohen a victory against Google, but also cleared the way for her to sue the blogger.

"The court also rejects the Anonymous Blogger's argument that this court should find as a matter of law that Internet blogs serve as a modern day forum for conveying personal opinions, including invective and ranting, and that the statements in this action when considered in that context, cannot be reasonably understood as assertions.

To the contrary, as one court in Virginia has articulated: "In that the Internet provides a virtually unlimited, inexpensive, and almost immediate means of communication with tens, if not hundreds of millions of people, the dangers of its misuse cannot be ignored.... Those who suffer damages as a result of tortious or other actionable communications on the Internet should be able to seek appropriate redress by preventing the wrongdoers from hiding behind an illusory shield of purported First Amendment rights."

Under this test, the difference between an opinion and a fact often comes down to a case-by-case analysis of the publication's context. In New York State, where Liskula Cohen's case was heard, the courts consider three factors in deciding whether a statement is a fact or opinion:

- Whether the specific language in issue has a precise meaning which is readily understood;

- Whether the statements are capable of being proven true or false

- Whether either the full context of the communication in which the statement appears or the broader social context and surrounding circumstances are such as to "signal . . . to the readers or listeners that what is being read or heard is likely to be opinion, not fact."

The decision removed the slanderous cave of anonymity that many bloggers have routinely abused on the Internet. The implications of this ruling, has now placed all bloggers on notice that they can be held responsible for their content should it be deemed libelous.

The decision should also serve to stem the tide of nastiness found throughout much of the blogosphere. It might also have a rebound effect of opening the door to others who feel they too have been unfairly libeled in blog posts.

When Cohen was asked why she didn't simply ignore the post made by the blogger she replied: "Why should anybody let it go? If somebody attacks somebody on the street, you're not going to let it go ... why should I just ignore it?"

Cohen told "Good Morning America" in an exclusive interview "I couldn't find one reason to ignore it."

In August 2008, the unnamed blogger wrote five different posts entitled "Skanks of NYC" on the Google-owned website Blogger.com.

Timeline of the case

- Aug 21, 2008: Post posted a series of nasty entries about model Liskula Cohen that were found to be actionable by the court.

- January 2009: Cohen files suit against Google demanding the firm release the name of the owner of the "Skanks of NYC" blog.

- August 2009: Manhattan Supreme Court Justice Joan Madden rules that Cohen is entitled to sue the blogger and that Google must reveal the person's identity to Cohen's lawyers.

- August 2009: Cohen announces she is dropping her plans to file suit against Post after Post's name is revealed.

- August 2009: Post announces she is suing Google for $15million for failing in its, *"… fiduciary duty to protect her expectation of anonymity."*

Steven Wagner (Cohen's Attorney) said that this case wasn't a matter of someone simply expressing the blogger's opinion. "One of the things that the judge did was balance the First Amendment Rights with the Rights people to be protected from harmful defamatory speech. It's sending out a message that the Internet is no longer a safe harbor for defamatory language."

This is one of the golden rules of defamation law: opinions are not actionable. The tort of defamation consists of harming a person's reputation, by making *false statements of fact* about that person. Note that key word: "fact." This means that statements of personal opinion are by and large safe from defamation claims. In model Liskula Cohen's case, Rosemary Port's blog apparently had posts referring to Cohen as the "skankiest in NYC" and a "psychotic, lying, whoring . . . skank." Another post stated "desperation seeps from her soul, if she even has one."

Parse those nasty statements a little bit, and you can see what got Port in trouble here. "Liar" and "whore" are two words that clearly make assertions of fact about a person, and very negative ones at that.

These are the kinds of statements that defamation suits are made of and that undoubtedly supported the order requiring Google to out the then-anonymous author.

Cohen's case is proof that despite the fact that we cannot sue Google, we still have a legal leg to stand on when it comes to suing the anonymous attacker. Cohen faced an enormous uphill battle in her quest to bring this matter to the Manhattan Supreme Court.

The biggest challenge was that she was a public figure suing for what appeared to be an issue of free speech, but Judge Madden obviously felt that this blogger had crossed the line.

What I find regrettable in this matter is not that Cohen won, but rather how having considerable wealth increases your chances of having your day in court. In this case, Cohen had pockets deep enough to get the attention of the courts. Every day thousands of Americans have to deal with Internet slander in one form or the other, but many of us can't afford to use our hard-earned money to battle it out in court.

> *The Cohen versus Google case is very similar to the movie Independence Day in which the nations of the earth battled the alien invaders to no avail for two thirds of the movie. Then one day a discovery was made that provided a way to bring down a seemingly invincible monster.*

As we examine the Cohen case it does give us hope that under certain circumstances you can root out those that hide in the shadows and spew defamatory comments all over the Internet.

We now know that Rosemary Port is the blogger that Cohen referred to during her ABC interview. In compliance with the court order Google was forced to release her IP address and e-mail address. Way to go Liskula!

The Cohen versus Google legal battle has been officially put to rest with the release of the blogger's name, and Cohen as has expressed no desire to sue Rosemary Port for damages.

Despite the fact that this case will probably have no bearing on the rest of the country because the ruling was handed down by a State Judge, we will still claim this ruling as a victory for the victims of Internet slander.

This case has taught me that we still have to place the blame and liability of Internet slander at the doorsteps of entity that created the immunity for the bloggers, Congress is truly guilty as charged.

At some point Congress will have to revisit the idea of allowing certain Internet forums to operate as pockets of slander and defamation.

The Cohen's case is proof that there are still little victories that we can win in our fight to hold those accountable for their lies, and their insidious blogs. One blogger asked, *"should we now be concerned that we could be sued because of this ruling for simply voicing our opinion?"*

I think that the Cohen's case proves with overwhelming clarity that what you do in the dark in an attempt to destroy someone's online reputation, can lead to you getting exposed and held liable in the bright lights of our legal system.

CHAPTER 6

You Have the Right to Defend Yourself

⧫⧫⧫

I do not think that there is any other quality so essential to success of any kind as the quality of perseverance. It overcomes almost everything, even nature.

⧫⧫⧫

Many of the people who have contacted me over the years to help them remove negative online links had no idea that they had the right to protect themselves from Internet slander.

Sure you can pay a Reputation Management Firm to do the work for you, but the purpose of this book is to teach you how to defend yourself from online slander.

The first step in protecting yourself is to embrace the fact that no one has exclusive rights to the first page of your search results. Google has maintained its position that it is merely a service provider, thus shifting the liability of the posted content to the third party that served as the publisher.

Since this is their position, my goal is now to teach you how to become your own publicist. The reason I want you to become your own publicist is because I want you to control the information that is visible about you or your business. Once you learn how to control the visibility of online information, it will then empower you to control your first page search results.

It is very important that you begin to take control of your brand. Your brand is your name, and your name is in fact, your brand.

> *Most people only think of a brand in terms of national brands like Ford, or GEICO, but any online attack against your name or the name of your business is an attack on your brand.*

One of the main points that I want you to get from this chapter is that you have a right to protect your name. I want you to approach your online reputation with the boldness of knowing that you have just as much rights to your first page search results as the person who attacked you.

The Tools of the Trade

I opened this chapter by placing emphasis on the need for you to become your own publicist. Before I get to far ahead myself please allow me to explain what I mean by become your own publicist.

Webster defines a publicist as - *an act or device designed to attract public interest; specifically: information with news value issued as a means of gaining public attention or support b: the dissemination of information promotion material c: paid advertising d: public attention or acclaim.*

I know you're probably already asking yourself the question "why would I want to attract attention to myself at this time?"

This time is perhaps the absolute best time to attract positive attention to the first page of your search results. Please keep in mind that there is only one way to remove a negative item from the first page of Google, and that is to have the negative link compete against other relevant links that would also like to be on the first page.

In some very rare cases you may contact the hosting company of the site and ask them to remove the site due to slander our trademark infringement; however the majority of the time this is very difficult to accomplish.

A simpler way to deal with the negative links that have taken permanent residence on the first page of Google is to publish your own content that will completely contradict the negative items listed under your name.

To become your own publicist means you will become active in publishing positive images, articles, and publicity with the intent of changing the public perception of either you or your business.

I discovered this principal very early in my career in the field of reputation management and brand protection. My first client only had one negative item on the first page of Google - that was the good news. The real problem was everything else on the first page of his search results had no association to him.

So in this particular case I had to basically create a positive image for my client, while at the same time, get my positive content to replace the negative content.

Believe it or not, reputation management is not an exact science because we are still at the mercy of the engineers at Google. There have only been minor advances in the techniques used to remove negative items out of view, but what has changed has been the strategies required to keep those positive links permanently in place.

So my first game plan was to simply develop a roster of different sites and publications that I knew would automatically land on the first page of Google.

To become your own publicist you will need to know how to get news about your brand out to the general public fast and effectively.

Your goal is to flood the first page of Google with the information that you want visible to the public.

Please don't get too concerned about how high the items land on the first page. Some of your positive content may not land above the negative link, but your goal here is simply to land your content either on or somewhere near the first page.

With use of high page ranking article sites, press release sites, document upload sites, and social networking sites you will develop the ability to saturate the Internet with your message.

The ability to attract a large amount of press coverage and media attention is a very powerful tool, especially when it comes to promoting yourself.

Many of times we rely on journalist to discovery our content or brand and hope that they would find it interesting enough to write about it. What if you could get them to come to you for information about your brand?

Don't worry, in our strategy section I will teach you how to use press releases to attract national attention, while at the same time dominate the first page of Google.

The Power of Your Name!

At this beginning stage I need you to realize the power of your birth name. George Forman and Michael Jordan mastered the art of branding their birth names, and your name has that same branding power. Just like George Foreman, you have the right to promote your name/brand as much and as often as you like in order to get your message out there.

The challenge of relying on a third party to publish your message is that you're leaving your brand up to their own interpretation.

A true publicist will always control the information, and the image of their brand. A precise publicist is always concerned about how the message will impact their targeted audience.

A really good publicist is a master at creating hype prior to the launch of the brand, you are now that brand.

With all of the above information that I just provided you, let us now think of yourself as the brand that we are going to launch.

In our strategies section of this book you will learn the power of a press release and article distribution. Our goal with the use of the press releases is to use Google against its self in a way that removes the negative items off the first page of your search results.

In the last chapter I shared with you how *Content is King*. Since Google is in love with new and relevant content, we will now provide them with an unlimited supply of new and relevant content about your brand. We will provide Google with a constant source of content released every week, all directed toward accomplishing one goal which is the removal of ugly items.

Not only will we use Google against itself in content, but we will also use it against itself in policies. Google has maintained a position that it will not get involved or sensor content posted by a third party.

With that understanding, it is our expectation that they will remain neutral as we publish positive information about you or your brand.

Now that you know that you have the right to publish positive information about yourself, I would like for you to take this opportunity to plan a strategy for your first page results. It's not enough to just publish items only because you have the ability to do it, everything that you publish should have a common theme and target.

If you have purchased this book because your business has come under attack, then I want you to publish content that is relevant to your business or your industry.

Another really good strategy for your first page search results is to begin to gather a few of your customer testimonials and publish them in a separate website.

Please absorb this one fact from this chapter if nothing else, no one has exclusive rights to the first page of your search results. And just as you would vigorously protect your Social Security number against identity theft, you should all so protect your online reputation with the same intensity.

Online reputation management is something that you should engage in even if you have never been attacked by an online terrorist.

The reason your online reputation is so important is because the information located on the first page of search engines can affect how people perceive you.

In public-relations there is a saying that "It's not who you are, but who people think you are that really matters."

I know that may sound a little superficial and shallow, but this is the world that we live in. Just about any contact you develop or potential client will search your name in Google. This fact is not a possibility, but a probability.

Take Control

I've had clients to tell me that the reason they never addressed the negative items in Google was because they were under the impression that the items would simply fall off the first page.

The interesting thing about this theory is Google is committed to indexing an item forever, which means that it will never fall off the first page on its own.

The only way to remove a negative item off the first page of Google is to attack it. You will have to go after this item with a hell's fury of punches designed to bury the link on lower pages.

If you were to examine the organizational structure of major corporations then you would discover designated departments committed to the protection of their image and brand.

You will have to become your own public relations department to defend your brand from online attacks.

Let's Get Started.

CHAPTER 7

Know Your Enemy

ഇരു

***If you only knock long enough and loud enough
at the gate, you are sure to wake up somebody.***

ഇരു

If your plan is to remove a negative item off the first page of Google then you will definitely need to unearth as much information as you can about the link.

Not only will you have to conduct extensive research on the link, but you will also need to stay up-to-date on Google's hot indicator of the month.

I used the term "hot indicator of the month" because Google constantly changes the criterion that determines the ranking of a website.

When I first started with SEO everyone was raving about the power of keyword strategies.

Then one day a few SEO guys figured out how to stuff multiple keywords into one site and Google devalued keywords as a primary indicator. As of now, Google has come full circle in its policy of determining how a website will rank. The term PageRank is Google's patented system of ranking a website based on a set of published and unpublished variables.

According to Google's own account:

PageRank reflects our view of the importance of web pages by considering more than 500 million variables and 2 billion terms. Pages that we believe are important pages receive a higher PageRank and are more likely to appear at the top of the search results.

PageRank also considers the importance of each page that casts a vote, as votes from some pages are considered to have greater value, thus giving the linked page greater value.

We have always taken a pragmatic approach to help improve search quality and create useful products, and our technology uses the collective intelligence of the web to determine a page's importance

There is one term hidden in the above paragraph that is king of the jungle, "vote." The term "vote" can be translated into the more common term known today as Back Links.

Back Links are now king, the more relevant links you have the higher your site will climb in search engine results.

But what are Back Links?

Without boring you too much with all of the inner workings of the algorithm, I would rather place the concept of back linking right where you can reach it.

Every time the URL of a website is embedded within another relevant site, that placement will count as one back link. Now before you nod off to sleep please allow me to explain how all of this is connected to the negative link located on the first page of your search results.

The more relevant back links a website has, the higher it will climb in page ranking. Notice that I keep repeating the term "relevant back links." A back link counts as one popularity vote, but that vote will only matter if the site where the link is embedded has something to do with the theme of the linked site.

Here is the part that has something to do with you; you will need to the how many back links your negative site has in order to beat it. Don't worry about trying to figure it out because I have already listed a few free sites that will help you determine the back links of your attack site.

Free Backlink Checkers

www.iwebtool.com

www.checkbacklinks.net

Before you can even think about removing your negative site off the first page of Google you will have to search the URL in one of the back link search sites.

Once you have determined how strong your attack site is, only then you will be able to plan your strategy.

Here is the Good News

The attack site appearing on your 1st page probably has only a hand full of back links if any. The reason is because people who post attacks on sites like Complaints Board simply post and forget about it.

In order for your attack site to increase in strength then the URL from that site will have to appear on other relevant sites. Chances are you are only up against a site that only has one to three back links at the most.

If you have encountered an attack site that has more than 20 back links, then you definitely have a very aggressive attacker on your hands. Having a negative site on the first page of your search results with more than 20 back links is not the end of the world, but you will definitely have to roll up your sleeves.

Keep in mind that Google is always adjusting different aspects of its page ranking strategies, but back link building is the one thing that has remained consistent.

Once you understand the basics of back linking, and how to build solid back links to the sites your targeting, it will not matter how often the rules change because you will remain within the core of Google's Page Ranking System.

The Insight of Alexa

Another site that I want you to become very familiar with as you initiate the discovery phase of your removal strategy is Alexa - www.alexa.com.

Alexa has comprised its own system of ranking websites according to the popularity and depth of the website.

SEO experts often debate on how much of the information from Alexa rankings are considered by Google because the indicators seem to coincide.

How to Use Alexa to Your Advantage

I am a really big boxing fan so for this section I want to use the analogy of a boxing match in which you are one of the boxers, and your opponent just happens to be your negative attack site.

I am not sure if you have ever noticed that before the boxers even step into the ring, the first thing that has to happen is both boxers have to go through a process called weighing in.

During the weigh in both fighters receive detailed information about the person they are scheduled to fight. Having this information is crucial because it allows both fighters to strategize against their opponent.

So here we are at the official weigh in of your heavy weight fight.

How much do you know about your opponent?

How much does your opponent weigh?

What is the success rate or the record of your opponent at knocking out other fighters in your weight class?

Alexa's website is totally free and collects information about the size, reach, and traffic flow of just about any website that's been published. How this information will help you is that it will provide you with what is known as an Alexa's Ranking Number, and a Traffic Rating.

Google also has a system very similar to the Alexa Rankings therefore the stats you receive from Alexa will help you determine how the site will also list in Google.

This is the part where we size up our opponent (the negative listing in Google) to determine what our punch strategy will consist of. In this example I have typed in a really common attack site known as Rip-Off Report.

Any site can move to the 2nd page of Google if you are determined enough to move it. For my example of an opponent I selected one of the more difficult opponents to fight.

The reason why the Alexa ranking is so high for this site is the number of people viewing this site each day, and the amount of high ranking sites connected as back links.

Lately I have noticed that Rip-Off Report page ranking is decreasing in strength and this is due impart because the site was downgraded by Bing, Yahoo, and partially by Google.

The Rip-Off Report is responsible for about four out ten calls we receive daily at RemoveSlander.com.

In sizing up this opponent I discovered in previous research that this site is in the reputation management business or SERM – Search Engine Reputation Management.

Knowing this information helped me to understand why the Rip-Off Report could care less if the information submitted about you was true or false, the fact that you were reported to their site gives them another prospect to market.

From a business perspective this concept is brilliant, but from an integrity and creditability standpoint, the Rip-Off Report is filled erroneous claims.

Lace Up Your Boxing Gloves

In sizing up my opponent I now know the ranking of the site and the total amount of back links pointing back to the site. I also know that the site will post every claim submitted regardless of the validity of the claim just to make a profit.

Equipped with this information I will now devise a strategy to offset the damage to my brand caused by the person or persons who posted this negative information about my business.

There are ways to push this site to the second page without paying anything other than the cost of this book, and I will cover this strategy in the sections to come.

For now, we simply need to know how much resistance we will experience as we attempt to move the site off the first page of Google and other search engines.

So now we know what we're up against, and we are now prepared to enter the ring. Alexa.com and CheckBacklink.net have provided us with crucial information that will allow us to plan how we win this fight.

CHAPTER 8

Goons & Goblins

ଚ୍ଚାଠ୍ଚ

You've got to say, I think that if I keep working at this and want it badly enough I can have it. It's called perseverance.

ଚ୍ଚାଠ୍ଚ

Identifying the **Attack Sites**

A negative attack site can come in many forms, so in this chapter we will review a few of the sites most commonly used for Internet Slander.

If I may make one quick distinction, there are a few sites that have common uses however certain individuals have converted them into attack sites.

For instance, there are general-purpose blogs that have neither a negative or positive intent, they are simply tools.

And just like with any tool, if placed in the wrong hands it can cause a great deal of harm due to improper usage.

Listed below are just a few of the types of sites that we have battled over the years in an attempt to remove negative content from the first page of Google.

Online Newspaper Articles

Many of the clients who contacted me came under attack in the form of newspaper articles that have been published to the Internet and sit directly on the first page of Google.

Not every newspaper has a practice of publishing all of its content to the Internet; however when it happens it can definitely cause a tremendous amount of aggravation for the person cited in the article.

The most common section of a newspaper often published to the Internet is the crime section.

It did not take me long to realize that the newspapers and law enforcement are partners, and quite often collaborate their efforts to spread crime related news. A few of my clients have found themselves posted in local crime sections due to a DUI arrest. And to the horror of some of these clients not only was their names published, but it also included the mug shot from the night of the arrest.

Once a newspaper article resulting from an arrest has been uploaded to the Internet there is also the possibility that the mug shot will also get indexed by search engines.

Here is the good news, in my experience newspaper articles put up the least amount of resistance. In most cases the strategies outlined in this book has been successful in removing newspaper articles off the first page of Google within 72 hours.

Quick Note - Newspaper articles are very vain in nature and love the spotlight despite their lack of staying power; on occasion they will try to reposition themselves back to the top of the page.

Blogs

Blogs are like people, not all of them are bad. In your case someone used blogs to attack you, but more often than not this is not the intended purpose of a blog. I cringe every time I have to deal with a blog mainly because of the embedded comments.

Blogs are sometimes the weapon of choice for online terrorists because it is very easy to remain anonymous. One of the challenges in dealing with attacks from blogs is that they often contain very graphic comments. What can add to the difficulty in removing negative blogs are consistent comments from anonymous posters.

> *The "Content is King" principal still applies to blogs, therefore even though a blog may have very few back links it can still put up quite a fight when you try to remove it.*

A blog that has several comments can get mistaken by the Google Bot as a site with relevant content. I have discovered that the best way to deal with a negative blog is to publish more blogs.

With this strategy we basically create our own blogs with the use of powerful back linking strategies, and relevant content.

Most attack blogs have very few comments other than the original post that could make it easier to outrank. This can work to your advantage because most online attackers know very little about search engine optimization, which is essential to maintaining a permanent position on the first page of Google.

Other than Word Press, I have become very dependent on a blog service called Blog Talk Radio. I find that this service has the best user friendly interface to build a blog from scratch.

Using Blog Talk Radio, you can create your blog in minutes, and very quickly get indexed by applying the strategies found in the strategy chapters of this book.

Forums

Forums can present the same challenges as blogs with one major exception; they are even harder to remove. There is no other explanation for this other than the forum contains relevant content.

Whenever you encounter a forum that requires that all new members are subject to approval, this is an indication that this page was created for the sole purpose of attacking you.

Now if you have encountered a negative forum with multiple entries, the removal strategies are identical to one's used to address negative blogs.

I have often had success in creating multiple positive forums in an attempt to push off one negative site. In the strategies sections of this system, I will go into further detail on how to drive a negative site off the first page of Google by creating more positive sites.

Created Domains

A created domain can definitely become a major headache if the site has landed at the top of your search results. Whenever I encounter a client who has been attacked with the use of a created domain it tells me that this attack is very personal, and the attacker is very aggressive.

More often than not, created domains have very few back links and only partially connect to the brand or keyword, but the domain name is composed of the clients' name.

This is where the headache comes in. The Google Bot will place a creative domain relatively high if there are no competing sites, and the content is relevant to the keyword. If you are fighting a created domain then you will need to do a little research to determine the best punch strategy for your success.

As we review the created domain, we will also have to determine what motivated the attacker to create the site. In some cases their aim is simply to tell a brief story, and in other cases their aim is simply to promote the title of the page.

I find that created domains are very similar to drive-by shootings. After they have made their presence known, the attackers simply disappears. The benefit to you is once they have launched the site they simply crawl back into obscurity because they believe that they have been successful in humiliating you.

The best approach to this headache is to determine the strength of the site based on the number of back links and relevant content, and then create sites more relevant to the targeted keyword (your name).

Facebook and Twitter

Sites like Facebook and Twitter are primarily privately hosted sites. Many times clients come to us seeking assistance with removing a comment posted on a Facebook wall, which is unfortunately beyond our reach.

Here is the good news; Facebook has done a tremendous job of only allowing very basic information to get indexed by Google.

The only unfortunate part about subscribing to Facebook is that it will publish four to six of your friends' names along with your name on the first page of Google.

CHAPTER 9

Sexting Prevention

ഔറ

History has demonstrated that the most notable winners usually encountered heartbreaking obstacles before they triumphed. They won because they refused to become discouraged by their defeats.

ഔറ

The beautiful Beyoncé and the alluring Lady Gaga mega-hit "Video Phone" has reached a breathtaking peak of more than 20 million views on YouTube. The collaboration of these two superstars was guaranteed to produce a hit but was anyone prepared for the fall out?

In Beyonce's version of the "Video Phone" sequel there's a heavy emphasis on someone being able to see her while talking to her. Judging from the choreography that creates a sort of sinister erotic undertone, viewers get the impression that they will see something genuinely tantalizing on the video phone, and that's where the problem comes in.

According to The National Campaign to Prevent Pregnancy, Sexting has become a major issue for school officials and law enforcement across the country.

With the increased popularity of smart phones we have now reached the age of the Jetsons in which teens can view the person they are talking to in real time.

Something that was thought of as futuristic fantasy has now arrived with unprecedented side effects.

What works perfectly in the hands of adults can quickly turn illegal in the hands of underage teens. Sexting or sending nude pictures via a cell phone or over the Internet equates to participating in child porn, even if the sender and receiver are both 17 years old.

This is where the law has clashed with parents and school officials who want to deal with the issue of sexting without adding under age teens to the list of sex offenders.

The Facts on Sexting

Nearly 20% of teens admit to sending racy or naked pictures of themselves in text messages. According to a February 2010 PEW report, 73% of wired American teens now use social networking websites, a significant increase from previous surveys.

Another recent PEW report found that daily text messaging among American teens has shot up in the past year from 38% in February 2008, to 54% in September 2009.

And it's not just frequency - teens are sending an enormous quantity of text messages per day. Half of teens send 50 or more text messages a day, and one in three send more than one hundred texts a day.

Now take 20% of the teens who have admitted to sending racy pictures of themselves, and factor it with the 73% of teens who now carry cell phones, and the result is tons of naked pictures floating through cyber-space.

Many of these same teens are totally unaware of the consequences of sexting, which can be life altering. Sexting has led to child pornography charges against teens in 10 States and increases in the number of pending criminal charges continue to escalate.

Blame it on the Smart Phones

Smart phones are part of the reason so many cases of sexting are now making their way to the local court house. Cell phone technology has evolved with warp speed since 2001.

Today you can view the home page of Google exactly as it looks on your laptop.

The real threat to the innocence and privacy of our teens has come in the form of SMS Messages and Skype integration.

Whereas SMS video allowed the teen to only send a 15-second video, cell phones that offer Skype will allow real-time imagery.

Skype promotes the fact that their customers can enjoy voice and video calls to anyone else on Skype, conference calls with three or more people, and instant messaging with screen sharing.

The major challenge with this form of technology in the prevention of sexting is now a teen can send longer video clips, and allow multiple teens to join in on the same video call.

Skype has yet to allow a user to block the ability to take unauthorized photos, which means one of the teens within this group will have no way of knowing that their image is being recorded by multiple users.

Educating teens on the dangers of sending nude pictures via the Internet or cell phones has become so urgent that it was recently addressed by Congressmen George Miller and the Committee on Education & Labor.

There are three ways sexting comes to light:

1. The teenage relationship comes to an end, and the pictures are publicly posted out of revenge.

2. One teen shares the photos with a close friend.

3. The pictures are posted on a social networking site like Facebook or Twitter.

Songs like Beyoncé/Lady Gaga's "Video Phone" run the risk of sensationalizing Sexting in the form of video to video messaging. The music video for Video Phone even features men dancing with video camera like headgear as they promenade around Beyoncé.

One Click from Disaster

All it takes is the wrong photo posted on Twitter to get indexed by Google, and all parties involved could find themselves in a bad predicament.

The downside to Smart phone technology is that the phones are always connected to the Internet.

Within seconds a teen can receive a video sent to their smart phone and have that video uploaded to the Internet moments later. Skype technology has simplified the video to video conferencing feature to such a degree that it sets the stage for an increase in sexting cases.

Most search engines will move relatively quickly to remove explicit images of underage teens, but the issue arises when the videos are posted on privately hosted sites like MySpace.

Sexting is pornography, and becomes child porn if the images capture underage teens. The issue of teens sending inappropriate photos is still a matter that has to be policed by the parents of the teens in the photos.

My fear is that life will begin to imitate art in a way that could glamorize sexting and lead to the destruction of the online reputations of teens all across this country.

Every parent should take this opportunity to connect with their teens on the issue of sexting, and the potential future damage of engaging in the act.

Prevention

According to District Attorney Risa Vetri Ferman, there are a few strategies parents can use aid in the prevention of Sexting:

- Place the computer in a common room such as a family room, kitchen or living room - As parents we would not allow our children to bring strangers to their bedroom but when they are alone in their room with the Internet they can "hang" with any of the 1.67 billion people worldwide who use the Internet.

- Talk to your children about the dangers they face now and in their future. Make sure that your children know there are dangers they could face and what those dangers are. Don't forget to make sure they know how their activities could affect their future. For example, once a picture is posted on the Internet it can never be pulled back. What they post today may be found by an employer in the future.

- Become involved with your child's online activities. If your child plays online games, talk to them about who they play with. Ask if they chat with the other gamers and become familiar with the game site.

- Be reasonable with what you allow them to do. Don't just tell your children they can't be part of an online community such as Facebook. Often they will just open an account from another computer. It is better to allow it, set up the safety features you want them to have and monitor their activity.

- Never allow your child to have a telephone conversation or an unsupervised meeting with someone they meet online.

- Enable Internet filtering features if they are offered by your Internet provider. Don't allow your children to set up their own account unless you are with them and can have a say in what filters are being applied.

- Install monitoring software on the computers that your children use. Make sure you know what your children are doing, checkup often and discuss any activity that you find dangerous or objectionable.

- Know all of your child's screen names and passwords. Remember, you can't keep your children safe if you can't see where they go. You pay the bill for the Internet use, and you have the final word on how it is used.

- Remember that these rules apply to cell phones, gaming systems and many hand-held devices. Most kids today have cell phones with texting and camera functions. Many have complete Internet access. You need to check their text messages and pictures for "sexting." Sexting is being done by children as young as 11 years old. X Box, Wii and other game systems that connect to the Internet can have chatting and or Internet access." (http://www.timesherald.com)

I want to add one more tip to the list of suggestions provided by District Attorney Risa Vetri Ferman; Don't allow your child to have cell phones with certain types of cell phone technology.

Cell phones that feature video to video conferencing and Google integration will provide your teen with the capability of participating in sexting instantly. I know this suggestion may be very difficult for many parents to embrace, but in this particular case it's probably best to tell your child "you can't have it."

Even in cases where we had successfully removed online photos and videos from search engines, the video of the 15-year-old victim was still circulated from cell phone to cell phone throughout her high school. This is where the real damage is caused by sexting, once the video is sent it's out there forever.

Whistles, Bells, and Sirens

What if I told you that there was a way to be notified the moment your teenager's name hits the Internet without paying a monitoring company a monthly subscription, would that peak your curiosity? Introducing Google alerts, a free service that can send you e-mail notifications at the exact moment your child's name is published on the Internet.

Here's how it works, simply sign up for the service on their website (link provided on the next page), and indicate the e-mail address where you want your notifications forwarded. This service is extremely reliable. As a matter in fact I use it daily to manage the online reputations of many of my corporate clients.

This is not a service that Google advertises which would explain why many people are totally unaware that it even exists. Consider today your lucky day because listed below I have included the step-by-step instructions on how to create an alert for your child.

How to Create a Google Alert for your Child:

- Step 1 - Point your browser to the Google Alerts Page: www.google.com/alerts. Enter the keyword(s) for the alert that you want to setup.

- Step 2 - Select the type of Alert you want to receive. The comprehensive Alert retrieves news from blogs, news sources, Google Groups messages and websites. You can choose to get results from only one of these sources, instead of all sources.

- Step 3 - Choose how often Google will send the Alerts to you. Google can send your alerts as soon as it finds a match to your keyword, once daily or only once a week.

- Step 4 - Enter the e-mail address that you will use for your Alerts. If you don't have a Google email account, you will need to register for one.

- Step 5 - Click "Create Alert" when you are finished entering your keywords, choices of sources, and frequency for messages.

- Step 6 - Review and revise your Alerts if you receive too much or too little information. Log in on the Google Accounts page. Choose "Manage Alerts" to see your saved Alerts. Delete alerts that you no longer need (As provided by e-how).

Another wonderful benefit of Google Alerts is you can set up an alert for just about any keyword that you would like to monitor. It may also be a good idea to monitor your name as well as your business. If you have selected the name of your business, then any time your business name is published you will receive an e-mail notification.

This is the absolute best way to not only monitor the online activity of your teenager, but to also stay on top of potential threats to your teen's online reputation.

What I appreciate most about this service is that it will notify me in enough time to prevent a negative item from making its way to the first page of Google. This is indeed a powerful tool.

If a video or pictures of your child have been uploaded to the Internet (as identified by your child's name) you will receive your notification the moment that item is indexed by Google. Yahoo, and Bing both offer a similar service and I recommend that you set up alerts with their services as well.

As I continue to advocate for the safety of our youth in online environments, I ask that you take this moment to set up Internet alerts for every member of your family.

In our battle against cyber-bully attacks and online defamation receiving notification of a potential threat will help minimize the damage as well as decrease the time frame required to remove it.

I also invite you to visit our website www.RemoveSlander.com if you should find that you need additional resources in removing insidious content from the first page of your child's search results.

CHAPTER 10

If You Build It They Will Not Come Back

Our greatest weakness lies in giving up. The most certain way to succeed is always to try just one more time.

How to Build a Wall around Your First Page Search Results

In this chapter we will examine several ways of building a fence around your first page search results.

It is important to understand how backlink strategies will play a major role in not only removing negatives items from the first page of Google but also provide protection in preventing future attacks.

With the use of the back links strategy you will learn in this chapter, you will be able to identify positive links that are already visible on your first page search results, and increase the page rankings of those links.

There are reputation management firms that only practice content creation as their primary strategy in removing negative links. Although this strategy has shown promising results in removing less resistant links, the more aggressive links will still require a more permanent solution.

As I mentioned earlier, my goal is to increase your knowledge of SEO strategies that will give you a clearer understanding of how website rankings are calculated.

The first thing I want for you to do is to review your first page search results from the top which we will now refer to as the number one spot, all the way to the bottom which in most cases is the 10th link on the page.

At this point you may already have identified all of your positive links that are located on the first page. Once we have identified the positive links, we will now take those links and cut-and-paste them on to a word document.

One Quick Note - Typically Google will show 10 search results for any given keyword. One of its more common practices is to only allow one URL to occupy no more than two to three spaces on the first page.

You may have encountered this even when viewing your negative link because sometimes one negative site will have two links appearing, but both are connected to the same URL.

Once you have all of your positive links copied onto a word document, we will now examine a few strategies that will allow you to build strong solid back links to each of your positive links.

If the remaining sites on your first page search results have absolutely nothing to do with you or your business, then in our section on content creation we will cover how to land positive links on the first page.

How to Build Back Links for Your Positive Content

Here is why I am placing so much emphasis on building solid back links. Let's imagine that you have a negative item sitting in the fourth spot in your search results, but all of the links below it are all positive. If you apply the correct amount of back links to the positive sites just this simple step will begin to create movement on your first page.

In one of our previous sections I paused just for a second to drive home the point of creating relevant back links and here's why: the more relevant the back links that you build from the site, the greater the page ranking will be for that website.

There are at least three strategies that we will use to build solid back links.

1. Articles
2. Press Releases
3. Blogs

Using Articles to Build Back Links

One of the absolute best ways to build relevant back links is through article marketing. Article marketing is the process of creating content relevant to your website to drive traffic, create awareness, or simply build relevant back links. In your case, we will use article marketing as a way to build solid links in an attempt to strengthen our positive sites.

When writing an article with the intention of creating back links it is very important to use article directories which are considered to be high ranking sites. I suggest using some of the more popular sites like Go Articles, Ezine (which have the tendency to be very strict), and Articlebase.

When you submit an article to a site like Articlebase you will reap multiple benefits. The first benefit is most articles submitted to Articlebase will land on the first page of Google.

The second benefit is Articlebase offers its content at no charge to affiliate marketers which means additional sites will have access to your article, and the links you have embedded.

In our next section we will get more in depth on how to prepare the perfect article as a part of your SEO Strategy. For now I just want to keep it simple so that you grasp how all of the pieces will come together.

Using Press Release to Build Back Links

Using a press release to build back links is a great way of not only getting relevant links but also as a way of attracting national attention to your website. Press releases are not just for business use, they're awesome as a tool to update the world on your most recent activities.

One of the major benefits of using the more popular press release services is the opportunity to get included in Google News.

Getting included in Google News could mean more exposure for your press release, and additional positive links appearing in your search results. Typically press release sites offer distribution to other press release sites which creates the opportunity to gain additional back links.

The only downside to press release distribution if any would have to be the cost.

A decent press release can cost anywhere from $49-$350 depending on the distribution you have selected.

> ***Many press release sites also promote their distribution service as a way of building quality back links to your site.***

Listed below are a few of the press release sites that I personally have used and highly recommend for their ability to land on the first page of Google:

> *www.free press release.com*
>
> *www.onlinePRnews.com*
>
> *www.PRLOG.com*
>
> *www.freepressindex.com*
>
> *www.inewswire.com*
>
> *www.prweb.com*

All of the sites that I listed offer a free press release service which proves that you can build quality back links without spending hundreds of dollars. Submitting press releases for you or your business is also a great way to drive traffic to your website or E-Profile.

I know the primary focus of this book is to teach you how to remove a negative link from the first page of Google, but many of the same strategies can also help you drive traffic to your website and help you land under very competitive keywords.

The strategy here is very simple. The first part requires that you create a press release about news related to you or your business and embed one of the links from your list of positive sites.

To accomplish this you would first prepare the title and body of your press release. Once you arrive at the bottom (in the media contact section) of the press release include one of the positive links from your list.

Using Social Media to Build Back Links

Many social media sites have become a great place to build high ranking back links for your website. Social media sites are becoming my preferred place to build backlinks because of the speed at which the sites register.

By far social media sites will produce the greatest amount of back links in the shortest time.

There are two sites that I personally use because of their speed and the strength of their links:

www.pingfm.com

www.yedda.com

One of the greatest features of www.yedda.com is its sheer speed. Yedda.com is a questions and answers site, but it will also allow you to insert a link to your web site.

I have noticed the same link building power with sites like Yahoo Answers. This site is constantly crawled by Google which will allow you to quickly add back links to your positive sites.

PingFM.com is another one of those sites that will provide you with multiple benefits. Using this site can provide you with back links from social media sites that you have authorized PingFM.com to update.

How Ping works is it allows you to update all of your social media sites at one-time, thus creating links with every Ping.

Another residual benefit of using social media is the ability to build back links from social bookmarking sites. For some unknown reason Google has stamped a seal of approval on just about every social bookmarking site there is. Social bookmarking sites can provide you with back links that are both relevant, and permanent.

It All Connects to SEO

The Internet is constantly evolving.

Every month we see the release of hundreds of social media sites that are all trying to become the next Facebook. In the above examples the sites that I mention are highly effective today but could become irrelevant tomorrow. The goal of our theory is to not only teach you what works today, but why it works, and allow you to make adjustments as needed.

I also want you to become more assertive in finding new sites that will produce similar results like the sites I mentioned above. There is only one guarantee when it comes to understanding Google, the moment we think we have figured it all out, everything will change again.

There are some principles in SEO that will never change regardless of the shift in page ranking criteria. Regardless of any new trends or fads, back linking strategies will remain relevant.

Here is another fact that is very close to being a guarantee. As long as Google has an insatiable appetite for new content, you can count on your press releases & articles landing on the first page of your search results.

This is why I wanted to take this time to teach you the basics of SEO because these strategies will remain dominant players in the world of page rankings.

Every week you should actively publish positive content about you or your business. Every week you should submit at least one press release announcing some wonderful aspect of your professional career.

From this point forward, your goal is to make sure that negative content has no place to land on your first page and has to settle for page 5 of your Google search results. Once you have occupied all of the prime locations in search results with solid sites, then the only place a negative site can land is on the 4TH or 5TH page.

Coca-Cola is a perfect example of this strategy. The first page search results of The Coca-Cola Bottling Company represent the best case scenario of brand protection.

As we review the first page search results for Coca-Cola, one could get the impression that this brand is favored by everyone on the planet, but we know that is not the case.

The reason that all negative comments, links and blogs are missing from their first page is both deliberate, and preemptive.

Coca-Cola has gone to great lengths to protect their brand from online slander.

Coca-Cola is employing the same strategy that I am sharing with you in this chapter; you have to build a fence around your brand (your name).

Coca-Cola has been very successful in using Google against itself by making sure that every link that appears on the first page of their search results is connected to one central theme.

We can learn a lot from major brands like Coca-Cola and Ford, but simply knowing their strategy is not enough if you are not committed to doing the little things that make it all possible.

Build It Slow

I want you to resist the urge of going out and paying a company to add 10,000 back links to your domains.

Doing so can cause Google to penalize your site and prevent it from increasing in page rank and strength. This is why I suggested the use of article sites and press release directories as a way to build authentic and relevant back links. Your back links have to appear genuine.

A great place to start would be www.yedda.com. Yedda.com is constantly getting updated by Google because it provides a constant source of new content. Back links from this site are valued probably more than most social media sites, but even that is subject to change.

Trust me when I say this, Google has a way of knowing that you have used a service to add back links to your site.

Please do not confuse purchasing back links with paying for the distribution of your article or press release; these two are totally different.

When you're paying for back links what you are doing is paying for popularity. Google gets really angry when you try to manipulate their page ranking formula with fake back links, so please avoid this practices altogether.

Fly Under Radar

As you are trying to remove your negative link off the first page of Google, I need you to be mindful of not attracting unnecessary attention to your efforts. What I mean by this is certain types of Black Hat Strategies can tip off the engineers at Google, and cause them to flag your keyword (your name or business name).

Once your keyword has been flagged, any effort or attempt to improve your first page will encounter a roadblock.

As long as you do the majority of the work yourself and avoid outsourcing your SEO strategy then you shouldn't run into any problems. Like I mentioned before, the main thing that will cause an alarm to go off is purchasing a huge amounts of back links from blog mills.

I discovered firsthand what a Google slap feels like while trying to repair the online reputation of one of my biggest clients.

In an attempt to hurry up and get the job done, I tried to cut a few corners and the end result was the job took four months longer than it should have.

The goal of this section was simply to give you the foundations to build a positive image of your brand whenever your name is searched. The chapters to come will provide you with more strategies and details on how to totally lock the entrance to your first page. This chapter concludes the theory portion of this book as we now prepare you for the practical application of these strategies.

Ding! Ding! Ding!

CHAPTER 11

Fight Training

❦❧

Your chances of success in any undertaking can always be measured by your belief in yourself.

❦❧

Learning How to Fight Your Negative Content

Welcome to your Heavy Weight Fight Training Camp. I decided to name this book *"How to Fight Google and Win"* because it is going to feel like you're in a fist fight.

You may have noticed that at no point during any of the prior chapters have I ever said that your challenge would be easy, because it is not.

Google prides itself in being deliberately difficult to understand. Regardless of the claims of so-called gurus, no one has really cracked the code.

This is why I want you to really focus on how to work within their system versus trying to use black hat strategies that simply do not work.

The good news is there is no need to reinvent the wheel, because we have already discovered a few techniques that will work the majority of the time.

As you may have already figured out, I am a huge boxing fan; therefore I can find no greater analogy to use than a heavyweight boxing match. I want you to visualize your negative content as an opponent who has already demonstrated his intentions to cause you serious pain and suffering. We have now reached the middle of the ring and moments from now your fight will begin. Let us prepare ourselves to fight this negative site.

Types of Punches

As with any skilled fighter, you will have to become familiar with a punch strategy. In your case your punch strategy represents the type of techniques we are going to use to move the site off the first page of Google.

The following is a list of punches that we have decided will give us the best opportunity to win this fight.

Jab = Articles and Press Releases

Hook= Video Marketing

Straight Right = Created Domains

Uppercut = BLOG TALK RADIO Blogs

Body Blows = Adding Backlinks

Jab (Articles & Press Releases)

It's the same as if you are boxing a real opponent; the jab is an effective way to test the resistance of your adversary. Articles and press releases are very instrumental when used as your first wave of attacks on your negative site. Articles will typically land on the first page of Google for less competitive keywords; however they don't really pack a lot of bang with their punch.

If you have published an article and you notice that it has landed in the top five spots on the first page of Google then this is a really good sign, but please keep in mind that the fight is just beginning.

You really want to use articles and press releases as a test to see where your positive content will land.

Having said that, there are a few press releases that will permanently remain on the first page for less competitive keywords; however there is considerable cost involved.

Articles and press releases are indicators that will provide us useful information on how much work is going to be involved in defeating our negative site.

When it comes to using the jab I really want you to subscribe to some of the higher ranking sites like Article Base, Go Articles, Online PR News, and I-News Wire, just to name a few. I charge you to do your own research and find more sites that will help you accomplish your goal of landing on the first page of Google.

There are three major parts of your article that I want you to pay close attention too.

The first section of your article, and probably one of the most important areas to pay special attention to is the title of the article.

The title of your article is extremely important because it is the number one item that tells Google where to index it. I am going to keep this really simple, always place your name in the title of your article.

Regardless of what the press release is about, it is very important that your name is either in the beginning or at the end of the title.

One of the ways I accomplish this is by adding my name as the author of the article, for example;

How to Fight Google and Win by Tyronne Jacques

Notice at the end of the title I included my name. Even if you totally screw up the rest of the article, placing your name in the title will land that article somewhere around your first page search results.

The second area I want you to pay attention to as you prepare your article is the description box. The description box is important because it helps Google confirm that it has indexed this article in the correct place. The description box is where you will give a two sentence summary of what the article is about, for example:

How to Fight Google and Win by Tyronne Jacques is a step-by-step guide on how to protect your online reputation. This book is jam packed with strategies and techniques designed to help you remove negative content off the first page of Google.

The last section I want you to pay close attention to as you prepare your articles and press releases is the tags section.

The tags section is designed for you to input all of the relevant key words that are associated with this article or press release.

One of the more common practices for entering tags is to separate them with the use of a comma for example:

How to fight Google and win, Tyronne Jacques, how to remove negative articles, online reputation, how to protect your online reputation, remove negative content, Slander,

Notice my tags are nothing more than words that are found throughout the article or press release.

As you may have noticed, I often refer to certain items as relevant. Google determines what is relevant based on the tags/keywords embedded in the article or press release.

Many of the press release sites and article submission sites use the same format; therefore you can expect to see the same set-up over and over. Once you arrive at a site like Article Base you can expect to input the information into the following sections:

Title Box

Description Box

Tags Section

Article Body

Author's Information Box

> *Please do not overlook the author's box as you prepare your articles and press releases.*

The author's information box is normally located toward the bottom of your submission form. It is in the author's information box that you should include links to your positive sites.

The author's information box is what creates the back link from our positive website that we have created.

This all ties into our strategy of building relevant links that will increase the strength and page ranking of our website. The reason Google will consider this back link relevant is because the content within the article matches the content on the website.

Hook = Video Marketing

Video marketing has recently become very popular among search engine optimization experts for its ability to land on the first page of Google.

Many video marketing sites are now boasting that they have the capability to dominate the first page of Google. In my research I have found this theory only partially true and here's why.

Due to the popularity of YouTube several video sites have emerged in an attempt to either compete or coexist with their success. There are two sites in particular that have the extraordinary ability to land on the first page of Google.

Daily Motions and Meta Cafe are two of the premier video upload sites that seem to dominate Google's page rankings.

Similar to articles, videos sites seem to have a very short lifespan after landing successfully on the first page.

If you have ever uploaded a video to YouTube then there is nothing new that you have to learn because the process is exactly the same. The only thing that I want you to pay special attention to is the tags, title of the video, and the description box.

In our office we have a rule called the **ACL**, which stands for **A**lways **C**reate **L**inks. Just as the ACL Tendons are extremely important to the movement of your body, the same is true for the upward movement of your page ranking.

The first thing that should appear in the description box of your video is the URL of your website. Video marketing sites rarely include an author's box; therefore the one sure way of creating our back link is by including our Web address in the description box.

It is very important that you title your video the same way you titled your articles. Inserting your name in the title, description box, and tags will allow Google to determine where to place your video.

Straight Right = Created Domains

Our next punch is called a straight right which is definitely one of the more solid licks that we will throw. Created domains or registering domains is one of the best strategies for taking control of your first page search results.

Throughout this book I have talked about building that fence around your first page search results and this is how we will do it.

The first part of this strategy requires that you reserve your name as a domain name, for example;

http://www.tyronnejacques.com

In the above example, I have registered my name as a domain. This simple strategy will start the process of you taking ownership of your keyword, and your first page search results.

In the beginning of this book, we established that your name is your brand. The first stage of brand protection is to secure the rights to your name.

The practical application of this will require that you register your name today, if you haven't already done so. There are several services that I highly recommend to complete this step, Intuit Web Design and Go Daddy.

Taking control of our first page search results will not only require that you register your domain name but also create a webpage or profile page connected to that domain.

The fine folks over at Intuit Web Design have simplified this entire process by creating drag and drop templates that allow you to build your own website for free (however there are costs associated with registering your domain).

I really encourage you to become familiar with how to build your own websites.

There once was a time when building a website required that you learn HTML Code, but sites like Intuit have taken the headache out of the entire process.

Many of you will discover that the site that attacked you was a created domain, therefore the more you learn about how to create websites, the more you will be able protect yourself.

If you plan to build your own website then I need to introduce you to a term called *Meta-Tags*. The meta-tags are very similar to the description box of your articles.

This section helps Google and other search engines determine where to index your website.

The meta-tags box of your website should include a brief description of your website. This is the most important strategy as you begin the process of building your website, so please make sure you fill in the meta-tags box. Include your name in several places in the meta-tags and keyword description of your website.

Another helpful hint is to name a few of your web pages after yourself for example; instead of just simply calling it a Contact Us page, let's name it Contact Tyronne Jacques.

Little things like inserting your name in the title of your web pages as well as embedding your name in every little corner of your site will only increase your chances of landing site on the 1st page. Once you get the hang of building your own websites, set a goal to create three really unique sites that all have one thing in common, you.

Uppercut = Blog Talk Radio Blogs

Other than Word Press Blogs, Blog Talk Radio Blogs (www.BlogTalkRadio.com) will become vital tool in your fight against negative online content. The reason that I absolutely love Blog Talk Radio blogs is because of their simplicity, and their page ranking potential.

I started using Blog Talk Radio about nine months ago and many of those same blogs are already dominating the first page of Google.

Here is why you too will fall in love with Blog Talk Radio;

1. It's free!
2. You can get a really cool domain name very similar to your own name
3. You can create multiple BLOG TALK RADIO blogs
4. They are perfect for targeting other attacked blogs
5. The strategies in this book will teach you how to get index in Google within 48 hours

Creating your Blog Talk Radio blogs is the next best thing to registering your name as a domain.

It is very important as you're setting up your blog that you use your name as the name of the site.

Keep in mind that Google will determine the layout of the first page of your search results based on the relevance of the first 10 sites.

With this idea in mind we will now saturate your blog with content that will make it very easy for Google to index it on the first page of your search results. Once you have created your blog, I ask that you develop a habit of updating it with unique content on a regular basis.

Remember that Google has an insatiable appetite for content, therefore the more unique and relevant content on your blog, the higher your site will rank.

Body Blows = Adding Back Links

By now you should have a very good understanding of the importance of building solid back links, and how they are factored into Goggle's page ranking system. Back links are, in fact, a severe body blow to your opponent. The more opportunities you get to land this punch, the harder your opponent will fall.

I consider my opponent knocked out the moment the negative site lands on page four. Until we are able to achieve page four results we are simply winning the round, but not the fight.

Our **ACL** principal *(Always Create Links)* is at the core of our back linking strategy. Articles, press releases, video marketing, and Blog Talk Radio blogs all require a substantial amount of relevant tackling to maintain their position on the first page of Google.

There are two quick points that I want to add to this section on landing solid body blows.

1. Placing your newly created domains in sites like Yedda.com will accelerate the indexing of the domain in Google.

2. Having your articles or press releases distributed to multiple sites is in fact the fastest way to build relevant back links

The heavy weight fight between you and this negative site is scheduled for 12 Rounds, each round in your case represents one week.

The more body blows you land on your opponent in the earlier rounds, the easier your job will be in the later rounds.

Our goal is to knock this opponent out by the 4th round. If you take the time to become familiar with your punch strategy, then you will know which punch to throw at the appropriate time.

From this point forward at the beginning of each chapter you will see the different variation of the following Punch Combinations.

Jab = Articles & Press Release

Hook= Video Marketing

Straight Right = Created Domains

Uppercut = BLOG TALK RADIO Blogs & (SMO) Profiles

Body Blows = Adding Backlinks

Just like any real heavy weight fight, you must have a plan of attack or a punch strategy designed to defeat your opponent. As a boxer your fight strategy will change based on the opponent in the ring, so too will your punch strategy change depending on the type of negative attack you're up against.

Your long-term success will not be determined by how fast you can land your jabs (articles and press releases), but rather how well you have applied your body blows (adding back links). Every punch combination you create should include a body blow.

You are now about to move into the "How To" section of this book. At the beginning of each chapter I have provided you with the suggested punch strategy you will need to defeat your opponent. Please feel free to make adjustments to the punch strategy as you proceed into your counter attack against the negative site.

The punch combinations at the beginning of each chapter are only suggestions based on what is currently working, but feel free to put your own spin on these recommended strategies.

There have been times when all I needed was one simple jab (articles and press releases) to knock out my opponent in the 1st Round (rounds equates to weeks), but this strategy would only work on a certain percentage of opponents.

I have faced of a few opponents that required multiple punch combinations was well as eight complete rounds to remove them from the first page of Google.

Please do not get discouraged because of the amount time it's taking to you to remove the item, diligence is the key to your success.

Diligence = Success

I wanted to title this section diligence because no changes will take place in your search results without diligence. You may ask why clients hire Reputation Management Firms if they can remove the negative content themselves.

The reason is it takes a lot of work on your part to move a negative item off the first page of Google or any other search engine.

No one can control Google or what appears on the first page of Google but the engineers at Google. Having said that, you do have the right to publish information about your brand that you feel is more relevant than the negative items currently appearing on the first page.

One quick note before we get started!

From this day forward, try not to click the negative link or attack site in an attempt to view it. Every time you open your negative site it adds to the page ranking of that site.

The strategies found in *How to Fight Google and Win* are designed to out rank the negative items appearing in your search results and drive those items to lower subsequent pages.

By clicking on the negative links you will continue to give life to the attack site making it more difficult to bury. Please keep in mind that it is difficult to bury something that is still alive. Sorry for the dry humor, but I hope you get my point – leave it site alone and work around it.

CHAPTER 12

How to Remove Cyber-Bully Attacks

Straight Right = Created Domains
Uppercut = BLOG TALK RADIO Blogs
Body Blows = Adding Backlinks

As I watched the news last night, I became very heart broken over the recent bullying case in Massachusetts that led to a teen committing suicide. It was such a senseless loss of life all resulting from a cyber-bully attack, especially since it could have been prevented.

As I ponder over why these kids tormented this beautiful young lady relentlessly, I also came to the realization that children have always been cruel. As far back as biblical times we find Abraham son's Isaac *and Ishmael* having to be separated because of taunting and bullying, taunting is definitely not a new epidemic.

I can remember back in high school in the late 80's kids were probably just as cruel as they are today, but every generation believes that this current generation is the worst. Here is perhaps the one major difference between bullying in 1989 and bullying in 2010; the Internet.

Like many of you I am also the parent of a teen and I recently had the bullying conversation with my daughter.

I wanted to know if she was being bullied or was, in fact, the bully of her school. If your child is not being bullied then consider yourself blessed, but also use this opportunity to find out if your child is bullying someone else.

It is very important to ask your teen if he or she is ganging up on another child simply because the group decided that it's cool to dislike a fellow student.

You may also uncover some vital intelligence that could lead to you protecting another child who has yet to notify school officials that they are being harassed.

Google has created an environment whereas anything goes, no matter how many lives are destroyed in the process. So the lies that a fellow cheerleader posted about your daughter will remain there every day for the world to see.

Imagine how your daughter feels knowing this information is on the first page of search engines and occupies the number one spot whenever her name is searched.

Once someone has posted a lie about you on the Internet it will remain there unless something comes alone and competes for the location of that item. So now imagine that someone has posted that your 16-year-old daughter is a slut, at the same time she is applying for college admission at a very competitive university. You have now entered The Wild-Wild West known as Google.

Cyber-bully attacks are now becoming more common with the use of sites like Facebook and Twitter. Regardless of the fact that the majority of the cyber-bully attacks take place during after school hours, the root of the attack is planted during school hours.

Many of the cyber-bully attacks that I have battled over past two years all stem from altercations that started in the hallways of the high school.

The challenge for many parents of teenagers is the reality that the teens know more about the Internet than their parents.

The consequence of this disparity can often lead to a parent discovering cyber-bully attacks weeks or even months after the bulling has already escalated.

What adds to the challenge of combating cyber-bully attacks is lack of predictability because the attacker are often very aggressive.

Recently we have witness every type of cyber-bully attack from the traditional arguments that take place between two girls competing for the attention of the "cute guy," to the recent case of an adult posing as a teen in an attempt to torment another teenager.

Cyber-bullying attacks are as random as terrorist attacks and can be just as damaging.

The issue of student cyber-safety and cyber-bully attacks has even gained the attention of Washington, DC as the House committee on education and labor held a hearing on cyber-safety.

The hearing was organized as a fact gathering session as the ESEA (Elementary Secondary Education Act) takes shape.

The House Committee meeting featured Dr. Phillip C. McGraw PhD who provided expert testimony on the damage caused by cyber-bullying.

Cyber-bullying will remain center stage as the alleged attackers will soon stand trial in the case of Phoebe Prince, (the Massachusetts teenager who, after being harassed, mistreated and then cyber-bullied for three months by a group of girls, hung herself in a bedroom closet).

During Dr. Phil's expert witness testimony he went into details of how cyber-bullying is an increasingly threatening epidemic, and a leading cause of suicide amongst teens who fall victim.

"We must change our sensitivities, our policies and our training protocols so we do not let the victims of today's 'keyboard bullies' fall through the cracks. That is why I am here today to suggest you add language to address cyber-bullying to the Elementary and Secondary Education Act."

"A cyber-bully in 2010 has the weapons to cause pain and suffering to victims that no other generation has had to cope with."

What I find particularly interesting about cyber-bullying prevention is that the parents of kids who are not being bullied seem to show no interest in the subject until they are directly affected.

As a parent, even I had to address my daughter and her friends for isolating one little girl based on the clothes she wore to school. Your child may very well be in the "In Crowd" today, but tomorrow it could be you calling us to remove insidious comments posted online about your daughter.

According to the Cyber-Bullying Research Center, cyber-bullying victims are almost twice as likely to attempt suicide compared to those who have not endured such bullying. Just as shocking are the studies that show how little is done about what is happening.

As presented during the testimony by Dr. Phil, it is estimated that 85% of bullying today goes on unabated. Because cyber-abuse almost always happens off campus, teachers and school administrators say they have no power to intervene.

Because no "official crime" has been committed, the police say there is nothing they can do. And sadly parents are almost never aware of what is happening.

Listed below are six basic steps that you can take to help prevent cyber-bully attacks against your child.

1. Have your child take you to the sites they frequently visit and to show you what they do on those sites.

2. Have your child show you what they have in their profiles on social networking sites to make sure it is accurate and appropriate.

3. Scrutinize your child's friend's lists on their various accounts and make sure they recognize the identity of each friend.

4. Make certain that your child have never and will never share their passwords with anyone, even a friend, to avoid the risk of someone impersonating them.

5. Encourage school-aged children to change their password regularly.

6. Have a very pointed conversation with your teen about sexting - the risky practice of sending sexually explicit photos and/or messages which can

easily be forwarded without their knowledge. Doing so may be defined as child pornography.

Repairing the Damage from a Cyber-Bully Attack

There is only one major difference between a cyber-bully attack and the typical defamation attack that we encounter, Facebook! The majority of cyber-bully attacks will take place on Facebook in the form of comments posted on someone's wall. Facebook has really stepped up to the plate and implemented more security features that allow members to control the posting of comments on their Facebook walls.

Facebook has also done an exceptional job at preventing wall comments from getting indexed by Google. So now if your child is attacked within any Facebook forum, the attacks will remain relatively isolated.

The real challenge comes into play when cyber-bully attackers venture outside of Facebook to post additional comments on blogs and forums. Believe it or not teens have now created websites for the sole purpose of attacking other teens. If you have discovered that your child has come under attack then the first thing I want you to do is conduct your own investigation of each site that has published your child's name.

In a few instances we have been successful and contacting the hosting company of the negative site and asking them to remove the comments because the person involved is an underage child.

To find out which website is hosting a site publishing insidious content about your child simply visit www.whoishostingthis.com. This site is free and will provide you with the hosting company to contact with a Cease and Desist letter from your attorney.

If the site refuses to disclose the anonymous attacker, then consult your attorney about a motion to compel. Many of times a motion to compel is enough to scare attack sites into dropping the page that includes your child's name.

Search engines like Yahoo and Bing are leading the way in assisting parents with the removal of inflammatory comments about underage children. As always Google is tremendously slow and difficult to deal with when it comes to protecting the online reputation of minors. I can only hope that the legal pressure applied to Google in the case of Cohen vs. Google will also assist us in improving student cyber-safety.

Straight Right = Created Domains

If we are going to protect the online reputation of your teen then it is very important that we control the content visible on the first page of Google.

For a negative site to humiliate your child it will have to land on the first page of your child's search results.

Our strategy here is really simple - we must take up every available space on the first page of Google. To accomplish this goal, you will begin the process of creating a website and registering domains associated with that website. The ability to create and publish your own websites gives you a very powerful tool in the prevention of cyber-bully attacks.

By applying many of the strategies found in Chapter 8, you will not only be able to change the online perception of your child but also prevent any future cyber-bully attacks. Like I said earlier, the only way a negative website can humiliate your child is if that website lands on the first two pages of Google.

By creating positive websites that are properly designed you are, in fact, removing any and all available space for a negative attack site to land.

I know on the surface this may sound like a very difficult task, but services provided by Go Daddy and Intuit Web Design can help you build a website within two hours with the use of their easy-to-use templates. Many of these templates are already formatted, leaving you to only replace the generic text with relevant information about your teen.

Whenever I take on cyber-bully clients the first thing I do during my discovery meeting is try to get an understanding of the child's hobbies and afterschool activities.

I would then take this information and build several one page profile sites. I may even take a few pictures from my client's soccer game and using one of the templates from Intuit to build a profile page with the client's name as the domain.

Once you've followed the steps outlined in Chapter 8 you will then begin the process of getting this site indexed and on its way to the first page of Google.

The reason this strategy is very affective is Google is more likely to index and rank a domain name that includes the client's name.

Uppercut = BLOG TALK RADIO Blogs

Even if you decide to pay a reputation management firm to remove the negative sites about your teen, I promise you they will still use the same techniques that I am teaching you in this book.

The truth of the matter is the only way to remove something off the first page of Google is to replace it with something else. Google will still make the final determination, but if you play within their rules then you can tip the scale in your favor.

Take this opportunity to create a few blogs about your child which features the after school activities they enjoy.

One of the benefits of creating your own blog is that you get to control the comments posted to your blog. One of the reasons I suggest Blog Talk Radio blogs is because it gives the publisher absolute control over the content and the members of the blog.

To begin my strategy for removing cyber-bully attacks I would create the blog for my client and would then ghost write all of the posts for the blog. Depending on the extent of the attack on my client, I would normally charge anywhere from $770 - $900 per negative item. Reputation management firms can get rather expensive depending on the extent of the attack.

Most reputation management firms will not disclose their tactics until after you have paid your fee's, only then will you discover that you could have remove the items yourself. The reason we concern ourselves so much with the first page of search results is that studies have shown that most searchers only look as far as the middle of the second page. This is why my staff and I will only consider our efforts victorious if the negative item lands on page 4.

This is also a great opportunity to use the profile pages of social networking sites because of their ability to land on the first page of Google. With the help of www.pingfm.com you can update up to 50 social networking profiles at one-time

> *Another benefit to using a Blog Talk Radio blog is sometimes Google will index two URL's from this one site. Whenever this occurs the result could land the main URL directly above one of*

Our main objective here is to publish as much positive content about your child as we can over a 30 day period. In the beginning of this chapter I asked that you try to publish a least three sites your first week. Try to launch at least one website, one blog, and create your Pingfm.com account with positive content all targeted toward your keyword (which in your case is your child's name).

Body Blows = Adding Backlinks

Once we have created all of your positive content and have launched all of your sites, now is the time to lock your results in place. Our back linking strategy will basically remain the same regardless of how often we change the punch combination.

Think of your back linking strategy as the finishing touches on the fence you're building around your first page search results.

Unlike other forms of online slander in which there is hardly any day-to-day interaction, cyber-bully attacks receive a daily recharge because of your child's proximity to the attackers.

Every day presents new opportunities for arguments and hostilities that can take place during school hours.

The above reasons are why you should take this opportunity to build solid back links to your blogs, websites, and social networking profiles.

If you are battling a cyber-bully attack then you have to anticipate that you will come under attack on a constant basis.

With this basic understanding of your attacker, you will then have to commit to a weekly publishing routine. Listed below is an example of a full week of SEO (search engines optimization) activity.

- Monday - Prepare one article (400 words), using the keyword within the description and the title. Publish the article on article base, and article Blast directories. Cut and paste the content from your article onto your Blog Talk Radio blog. Finally submit the article you created to an article distributor like www.ContentCrooner.com which will distribute your content to 250 article sites instantly.

- Wednesday - Tweet the URL of your article in twitter as well as Ping the same URL including your keyword. Pinging your URL will also create additional back links once your social networking sites are indexed.

- Friday - Create a press release about the article you wrote on Monday in which you include the URL of your blog within the content. Constantly include the URLs of your blogs and your website in your press releases because in doing so you are increasing the page ranking of your sites.

At first things may seem a little tedious to you because of all the writing that is involved; however it will quickly become very exciting once you start to notice your content appearing on the first page of Google.

I can still remember the first time I published something and it landed exactly where I wanted it to go, that was truly an awesome feeling.

The reason why I invested so much time and energy within this one chapter was to empower you to take control of your child's first page search results. You can do this, just take your time and follow the strategies outlined in this book and in no time you will become your child's publicist.

The reason why cyber-bully attacks caused so much harm and destruction is because many people are totally unaware that they can do something about it.

I have now equipped you with every tool you would need to protect the online reputation of your child, and present them in a more positive light.

Just imagine the impression your work will have on college admissions counselors when they conduct their own vanity search of your child's name. Think of it this way, what your attackers intended for evil, you will now use it to create something positive and enduring.

CHAPTER 13

How to Remove a Negative Article

> **Jab = Articles & Press Releases**
> **Straight Right = Registered Domains**
> **Body Blows = Adding Backlinks**

Ding! Ding! Ding! I know we have prepared you for the worst case scenario, but negative articles are not necessarily in the category of the typical bad guys. In the Reputation Management business we have an unwritten rule against using the word "easier," but attack articles are nowhere near as difficult as forums.

The major headache you're going to encounter with a negative article is that they have the tendency to be redistributed to other affiliate websites. Online articles are typically derived from newspaper sites that also publish local news stories on their websites.

Only a few of the online articles will have comments posted about this story, other than that the article is simply a standalone piece of content.

There are a few quick observations that I want you to make as you begin to collect information about your negative article.

Is the name of your business or your name appearing in the title of the article?

If your name or your business name is only appearing in the description of the article but not the title then this will make the job to remove it less stressful.

The description of the site will carry far less weight than the title. If your name is appearing within the title of the article, then this will confirm that we will need a series of jabs and body blows in order to remove the site off the 1st page.

Is the article from a newspaper or an online article site?

Unless it is a newspaper like the Washington Post or the New York Times typically articles from newspapers respond well to jabs. I have seen on several occasions where the attackers would use an online article site to launch their attack; if you are noticing this then you're in a good spot. A URL for a site like the New York Times would have a tremendous amount of back links, but the one page on which your story is located may not have any back links.

The main point that I want you to grasp is this, outside of Google no one owns the exclusive rights to your first page search results. Your content has just as much rights to the first page of Google as your attacker, so let's exercise that right.

Punch Strategy

Listed below you will find a step-by-step approach to implementing your punch strategy. Our goal with this strategy is to remove your negative article from the first page of Google and other search engines.

Step One- Publish one article using two of my favorite sites www.articlebase.com, and www.prlog.com. The purpose of these two articles is to determine how much resistance we will face before we launch the rest of our counter attack. Typically both of these sites will land on the first page but how high they land will let you know how determined the negative site is to remaining relevant.

Remember that it is very important to insert your name or your business name into the title of the article, doing so will convince Google to index the article under your name.

Like we said in an earlier chapter the only reason this site hung around this long is because there hasn't been any competition for the first page. With this strategy we will create that competition.

Articlebase and PR Log.com are free services. With the use of these free services we will gain a better perspective on the type of effort that will be required prior to paying for more expensive press release services.

Because you're considered a new member your article may be subject to a 72-hour review before it is published.

One tip that will help you get quick approvals is to make sure that your articles are general in nature (not sounding like an ad or sales pages), and keep your links only in the author's box.

After the 72 hour period has passed and you notice that both of your published items are now located near the negative item, you will repeat this step using the sites that we have suggested. If you have noticed that none of your material has even landed on the first page of Google, then it's time to incorporate step two.

Straight Right

Step Two - We will know throw our straight right punch at the negative item on the first page of your search results.

The straight right requires that you register and create domains for the sole purpose of landing them on the first page of Google.

The theory behind this strategy is to flood our 1st page with relevant content that will aid in punching out the negative content.

Creating a custom website is an awesome weapon to use in your counterattack.

A custom website gives you many advantages like:

- The ability to publish an endless amount of content.

- The ability to create sub domains that can also get indexed in search engines.

- The ability to publish PDF files from your site.

To register a domain you will have to use services like Go Daddy or Intuit Web Design.

If you're a business owner I suggest that you register multiple domains for your current website. If you do not have a website, then this is a great opportunity to launch one. The purpose of the straight right strategy is to take up as much space as possible on the first page.

The more domains we register and get indexed into Google, the more space we will eventually take up. You may also want to consider creating multiple profiles on social networking sites because of the page ranking of SMO (Social Media Sites).

There are services that can create a profile for you on multiple social networking sites, for a small fee. The benefit of using these services could mean that multiple profiles will start to appear on the first page of Google and compete with the negative site. This will also be a good time to consider a site like Twitter because of its ability to index Tweets.

Once we have launched multiple sites all geared toward the first page of your search results, it will then become very difficult for that negative site to hold its position.

Step two is not designed to exclude step one, but to work in conjunction with each other to spur activity and movement.

Here is the reality of your situation; it is not the content posted on the negative site that I want you to become focused on but rather the location of the site.

Google will allow 10 items to appear on the first page of their search results.

Now some items are allowed to appear twice with the use of two separate URL's, but the general rule leaves 10 up for grab.

The design of our punch strategy is to land the jabs as well as the straight right.

Once our articles and registered domains began to land on the first page of Google, we will then begin to take control of our online reputation.

I suggest that you actively fight this opponent with a combination of jabs and straight right hand punches to set them up for our final punch which will be our knockout punch.

Body Blow

Step Three – Adding Back Links to the Positive Sites

The reason I want you to land your jab and straight right first is because it sets the stage for your body blow. Once your press release, articles, and registered domains have landed on or near the first page we can then begin the process of adding our back links.

The absolute best way to increase the page ranking of the positives sites you have just landed on the first page is to distribute your articles with the use of article directories. This is your opportunity to finally fight back against the negative site that has haunted you for so long. At this point we will strategically select the positives sites located directly under our opponent.

With the use of press release distribution and multiple indexed domains, we will finally begin to add to the strength of our positive sites. I would ask that you repeat this punch combination in the same order that is recommended until the negative item is off the first page.

The advantage you gain in using the body blow is you can apply this strategy to any and every link in your search results.

You now have the power to identify a positive link on your first page and then add to the strength of that link. This practice is both legal and ethical because you have the right to promote your positives.

I want you to get into the habit of creating domains and with the use of body blows strengthen your positive sites with links. If your website is at the top of Google under your keyword and you have concerns about that site moving, I would suggest that you spend the first week applying back links to your own website.

I have had clients express concerns about the main website moving out of the top place due to all of the SEO activity.

Once I was aware of their concerns, I then concentrated on making sure their primary site remained locked into place by starting my punch strategy one to two weeks later.

This punch strategy is definitely guaranteed to create positive content about you or your business. Soon you will be able to find other ways of benefiting from this one particular strategy because it is a gift that will continue to produce positive press.

Once you have removed the negative article off the first page of Google, I would suggest that you repeat this punch strategy on the second page.

Landing a negative item on the second page is still not far enough, because potential customers will search as far as the middle of page two.

Very few people will even consider search results on page three, but just to be on the safe side we should continue this effort until the negative site has landed on page four.

Even I have experienced moments when it seemed like nothing was moving at all, so please do not get discouraged. Keep in mind that we are still at the mercy of Google therefore we still have to work with them to in order to accomplish our goal.

No one fully understands when Google conduct its crawls (designated time to index or update their search results) so you may run into these intervals when it appears that no movement is taking place.

If you find yourself within one of these dead zones simply continue with your strategy and the indexing will soon catch up to you.

There are a few sites that are fully exempt from waiting on Google to complete a crawl. Yahoo Answers.com and Yedda.com are constantly crawled by Google which means your link from this site will get indexed within 48 hours.

Every time you register a new domain, or launch a new website I recommend that you find some creative way of inserting that domain into either Yahoo Answers or Yedda.com. From what I can tell Google actively crawls both of these sites on a regular bases if not several times a day.

There have been times that I registered a domain in the morning and the sites were indexed in Google by 6 p.m. Like I said before, the good news for you is that articles can be very passive however you will have to put in a little bit of work to remove them. Unlike forum sites, negative articles have a tendency to continually fall to lower pages just from using this punch combination.

If you find that your article is proving to be a more formidable opponent then I recommend that you add additional punches from your arsenal of weapons.

Now Go Knock It Out!

CHAPTER 14

How to Remove a Negative Blogs & Forums

Straight Right = Created Domains
Body Blows = Adding Backlinks
Uppercut = BLOG TALK RADIO Blogs

I recently came under attack in the form of a forum so I decided to test a theory. I searched the Web address of the forum and joined the site as a new member.

What I wanted to know was if I begin to create my own thread in the same forum that attacked me which one would Google placed in my search results?

What I discovered was Google took the most recent posting on the site and replaced the negative attack. The only reason this method worked was because Google will quite often index the most recent content from a website.

Since Google only allows so many links to appear on the first page, I was very fortunate that they pull the positive post, and replace the previous negative entry.

When I noticed the positive post on the first page, I became very excited because I thought I had discovered the Holy Grail of Google Indexing, but when I tried the exact same strategy for another client my comments were never updated.

The only reason I wanted to share this story with you is because there is no method to the Google Madness. What will work perfectly in one scenario always seems to fall short the next time you try it. I have only enjoyed consistent results with a few techniques, but I have taken comfort in knowing that they will work the majority of the time.

This is why for your next two punches I want you to throw a straight right (create domains) and land some body blows (adding back links).

Blogs and forums can be a major challenge to move off the 1st page because of the amount of comments posted on the sites. Google will always consider blogs and forums above many other types of websites because they have the tendency to produce a steady flow of content.

Blogs and forums allow the host to remain 100% anonymous which explains why so many attacks come in the form of blog posts and forums.

Once someone has used a forum to attack the reputation of your business, it's time to stop shadow boxing and prepare to fight back.

Take It to the Street

In New Orleans we have a saying called "take it to the street." Take it to the street could mean a good or bad thing depending on how it is used. For example, if the party had reached a point whereas it was jam-packed and standing room only than the crowd was start chanting "take it to the street." This was the cue for the jazz band to bring the party outside. A negative meaning of taking to the street would involve an invitation to a fist fight, which would normally turn into a really big fight.

If you have been attacked by a blog or forum than then it is the equivalent of someone inviting you to "take it to the street" for a fistfight. Blogs and forums are stubborn, deliberate, and very resistant to anything attempt to move them out of position.

Whenever I encounter a blog or forum I immediately begin throwing my straight right.

With forums you have to outweigh them and compress the negative entries to lower pages in your search results. If the negative attack site has come in the form of a blog or forum then you will have to allow yourself time to deal with it.

There have been a few occasions in which I have witnessed a blog or forum drop off the first page within a two-week period, but quite often it will take four to six weeks. I'm not saying this for you to get discouraged, or make you feel as if your mission is impossible, but I will need you to have realistic expectations about moving a blog or forum off the first page.

The reason it will feel like you are in a fistfight with your negative blog is because it can reposition back to the top of your page. I have even seen times when the site was on page two for a three week period and then repositioned to number eight spot on the first page.

Once again, removing a negative blog or forum is not a mission impossible. To avoid the aggravation I have experienced in fighting blogs I ask that you follow a few simple steps.

Uppercut = BLOG TALK RADIO Blogs

In our planning for your Heavyweight Bout we noticed that your opponent has difficulty defending the uppercut.

The uppercut will become a very important punch in your combination of punches to knock out a blog or forum. With the uppercut I want for you to create two Blog Talk Radio blogs. If you were to set up your blog right now then you could have it indexed by this time tomorrow. Another really powerful blog is a Word Press blog. Despite the challenge would setting up a Word Press blog they are definitely the darlings of the Internet.

Creating multiple blogs about you or your business is, in fact, the first step to knocking out a blog or a forum. In this particular case you will have to fight fire with fire, which also means fight a negative blog with multiple blogs.

To remove a negative blog or forum off the first page of Google we will throw multiple uppercuts. Every opportunity you get for the first week I ask that you build a blog or set up a forum on a popular forum website.

Depending on where your negative item is located on the first page, will also determine how many blogs you will have to create.

If your negative blog is located in the number spot on the 1st page then our strategy would call for a combination of 7 created blogs and profiles sites.

Creating a blog is not really that difficult; all you're basically doing is setting up a profile and posting your first comment. To make your blog really focused and targeted, I ask that you write a 400 word article in which you use your key word multiple times.

I would also ask that you keep the title of the article short and 100% focused on your name or the name of your business.

Straight Right = Created Domains

In the earlier chapters we discussed building a fence around your first page search results. Our straight right is where we begin the process of building that fence. Holding true to our formula $T + N(C) = L$ (from the anatomy of an attack chapter) we will also create an enormous amount of competition for the available spaces on the first page of Google. **There has to be competition for the first page or the negative site will remain in position forever.**

Not only will we create an arsenal of blogs, but we will now point our registered domain toward a few of those blogs. All that's required to point one of your register domains toward your blog is to ask the hosting company to do it for you.

Once your registered domains are indexed by Google, we will then begin the process of getting all of the sites and domains to land on the first page.

> *The key to getting the blogs to land on the first page of Google is to make sure that the title of your blog entry is 100% embedded with your keyword (your name or the name of your business.)*

Having a blog embedded with the keyword in both the content and the blog title will only increase the possibility of the website landing at the top of Google.

Another great tool that you can use to minimize a lot of the work in updating and maintaining your blogs is Ping FM.com. The best part about PingFm.com is that it will allow you to update all of your blogs at once.

How it works is you simply type in your post and Ping will update all of your blogs and social networking sites simultaneously.

The more you update your blogs and forums, the more relevant it will remain to your targeted keyword.

Once you have established your blogs you can basically allow this process to run on autopilot with the use of Ping. I would ask that you also get into a habit of Pinging your registered domain names at least twice a week.

As you Ping your domains and your blogs always include your name or the name of your business at the end of each entry.

I recommend that you keep a record of all of your created domains, blogs and forums by tracking them with our *How to Fight Google and Win Workbook*. Now that we have landed our uppercut we have now set our opponent up for the final punch in this combination, the Body Blow.

Body Blows = Adding Backlinks

I remember in the mid-1990s there was this movie that scared the crap out of me called, "Sometimes They Come Back." This movie is right up there with many of the all-time scariest as movies ever produced, but who would have expected anything less from Stephen King. Just reading the title of the movie was enough to let you know that something really bad was going to come back, and that was the scary part.

By not taking the proper steps to build solid back links to the sites you have created could also leave the door open for something to come back! Few things are worse than busting your butt to remove the item off the first page of Google only to have it re-surface a month later.

Another way to look at back link strategies is to think of it as cementing your first page search results. If you're familiar with the process of drying cement then you understand the importance of molding it as it dries to create the desired form. Once you have published all of your blog sites and register all of your domains, it is now time to cement those sites onto the first page.

We will now use the back link building power of article distribution to lock our sites in place. The same article I asked you to write for your blog is now the perfect piece to distribute to other article directories.

With the use of a site like Content Crooner you will build hundreds relevant links every time you submit your article.

Before you begin to frown at the idea of having to write an article please keep in mind that all of your positive content has the potential to land on the first page of Google. You are now shaping and forming a positive view of your search results.

You are now controlling the information that is visible about your brand instead of leaving it to the negative site to define your image.

You can also use sites like Yahoo Answers, Friendster, and of course Yedda.com to quickly build solid back links to your blogs. I ask that you continuously publish at least two positive items per week related to you or your business.

The more content you publish, the more you will control what information is visible on the first page of Google.

A positive article really does have the power to contradict a negative article, just as a positive blog posts can offset the damage of a negative blog post. If writing is not your thing then fear not, because they are companies that will provide SEO articles for you.

Whenever constant writing became overwhelming for me, I never hesitated to contact my friends at WL Marketing (paid content writers) in order to catch a break.

Nevertheless, our goal remains the same, to saturate and dominate the first page of Google with content that we have approved and released.

That negative blog or forum should come under so much bombardment from your positive sites that it abandons the first page altogether. As with any real fight you must match their intensity with a greater intensity.

It is not impossible to remove your negative sites from the first page but it will require a tremendous amount of persistence. So I challenge you to use the pain and embarrassment you felt when you first noticed the attack as your fuel to remove it.

Please keep in mind that you have the right, the absolute right to protect your name or your business from Internet Slander

Now a go exercise that right!

CHAPTER 15

How to Remove a Negative Complaint Site

> **Jab = Articles & Press Releases**
> **Hook= Video Marketing**
> **Uppercut = BLOG TALK RADIO Blogs &**
> **Social Profiles**
> **Body Blows = Adding Backlinks**

Nothing is worse than having some rogue idiot posting lies and slanderous content about you or your business all over the Internet. With search engines like Google becoming more like giant verification sites, if someone never had the opportunity to meet you then they would believe the online slander about you.

The days of people sitting down and working out their differences are long gone. Now everyone rushes to Google to air out their differences. I am sure when Larry Page created Google he never envisioned that it would become a forum to sling as much dirt as possible at an opponent, or to simply complain about your most recent online purchase.

Sure there are companies that really need to be exposed, but in my line of work I mainly deal with the vicious attacks from online smear campaigns.

And don't even bother complaining to Google because they could care less if it's true or not. Google is a self-proclaimed archiving system; therefore this position allows them to stay in the middle of what is true or false.

I recently received a call from a client who was very angry about an entry that was appearing on the first page of his results. While on the phone with the client I Googled his name and there it was on the first line, Rip-Off Report!

The Rip-Off Report was written in a way that would have destroyed any opportunity of future business for my client. This particular Rip-Off Report was submitted under a fake name with no contact information to even dispute or resolve the complaint.

Personally I am all for notifying the general public of businesses and individuals that rip off innocent consumers - this is not where I have an issue with Google.

The major issue I have is when you have a legitimate business that has come under attack from a competitor without anyway of dispelling the lies or revealing the truth. This is the worst case scenario for a business owner, especially if his business involves bidding for contracts.

I explained to the client that complaining to Google is an immense waste of time and his best option would be to remove the Rip-Off Report as quickly as possible.

Google has become such a monster that if you are victimized by them your only recourse is to employ a similar strategy to offset the damage to your reputation.

Hook = Video Marketing

The latest craze on the Internet is also a great way to land targeted sites on the 1st page of Google.

A site that has an embedded video will land on the first page of Google in less than 48 hours after it is posted.

Don't ask me why, because I can't explain why video's out rank other content on the web, but they are in fact the new champion of page rankings. The viral video effect has saturated search engines as YouTube video's race to the top of search results.

Here is what I have been able to understand about the page rankings of sites like YouTube; their page ranking is enhanced by the fact that YouTube is owned by Google.

This well-known fact is great news for you because you will now use the strength of Google to work for you rather than against you.

For those of you who may not want to post a video on YouTube out of privacy reasons then you can always post a PowerPoint video (PPT).

Here is some more good news about viral videos; there are dozens of video sites popping up every day trying to compete with the popularity of YouTube.

If one uploaded video will appear on the first page of Google in less than 48 hours after it has been posted then imagine the effect of uploading your video to multiple tube sites?

A PowerPoint video can be a series of slides announcing your new website or a product or service. Keep the video to less than 3 minutes in length with your voice as the narrative.

During the video make sure you mention your brand at least once every minute because Google automatically creates transcripts of all YouTube videos.

There are two video marketing sites that I highly recommend because of their page ranking, and the speed at which they land on the first page of Google.

DailyMotion.com

MetaCafé.com

Jab = Articles & Press Release

Listed below are the two sites I want you to submit your first publications to as our 2nd punch in the strategy.

For the article, I want for you to post it at Articlebase. At ArticlesBase.com you can submit an article and literally have thousands of readers worldwide as your article gets syndicated across the globe.

For the press release, I want for you to post it at Free Press Release. Thousands of media editors, broadcasters, press journalists and freelancers come to this site for fresh news stories every day.

Any business can benefit from the potential media coverage generated from a well-structured press release.

With the help of Free-Press-Release.com, your release will be sent directly to thousands of important members of the media community without the high cost of hiring a PR agency.

The good news is both of these services are free and typically land on the first page of Google. Keep in mind that the title of your content is very important to getting your articles to out rank your complaint site.

As often as possible I ask that you use your name within the title of the article for example.

For the press release submission title:

"Tyronne Jacques Lectures on How to Write a Business Plan"

For the article submission title:

"How to Write a Business Plan by Tyronne Jacques"

Having your name in the title, content, and the resource boxes at the bottom of the article or press release will trigger all of the search engines to index your content under your brand name.

Just like with any heavy weight fight the majority of the punches thrown will be jabs and the same holds true in your battle against your negative complaint site. Use the jab (articles and press releases), as often as possible to remove your complaint site. The jab is a great punch to set the stage for the lick you're really trying to land, the uppercut.

Uppercut = BLOG TALK RADIO Blogs & Social Profiles

In Round 1 we basically sized up our opponent by collecting some crucial information like the weight of the opponent and their success rate at knocking out other boxers. As your coach I want you to acknowledge the size of this opponent and not box him head-on or by standing directly in front of his punches. What I mean by this approach is that we are not going to contact the Rip-Off Report but rather work around them.

Contacting an opponent this big will only cause them to place more ads on the site that they launched to attack you. Once ads are placed on the site it will make it much more difficult to remove.

Once a negative site posts under your brand, it is basically there forever unless the publisher agrees to take it down.

Many of the sites like Rip-Off Report make their money from spreading negative information about you and then offering you their services to remove the negative posting.

So how about we never allow them to know how much this is upsetting you, let us agree to not contact them at all.

Instead of contacting them or having an attorney draft up litigation, we will employ a strategy in boxing known as the "Stick & Move."

The "Stick & Move" is used more commonly when one fighter chooses to throw a few punches and then back away from their opponent.

In the example using the Rip-Off Report, rather than contacting them (which would be considered standing directly in front of their punches) we will begin the process of using social networking sites to land your profile on the 1st page of Google.

Our uppercut involves the creation of profiles on social networking sites such as Twitter, Facebook, and Buzz.

It seems that everyone is using social networking sites these days; however you will use your social networking accounts as an additional weapon in the counter strike against your attacker.

In the chapter titled "Know Your Enemy," during the weigh in & size up of our opponent we discussed the Alexa Ranking system.

Well guess what the Alexa Ranking is for Facebook?

- Facebook - 2nd
- Twitter - 14th
- MySpace - 18th

The relevance of the above rankings should now be very clear; having an active account with all three of these sites will increase your chances of one of your profiles landing in the top spot in search engines.

Simply opening a social networking site is not enough to get your profiles indexed in search engines, you have to take 20 minutes out of your day and post comments to your site as well as link in with friends and colleagues to create recent activity. The best site from my prospective has to be Twitter for its ability to land positive comments on the first page of Google.

Body Blows = Adding Backlinks

Once again we will save the most powerful punch for last, The Body Blow. I'm not sure if you've noticed by now that bank linking is the most powerful punch in your combination.

I suggest that you focus your back links strategy on the video sites that have landed on the first page of Google. Video sites are the equivalent of a "one night stand" if you fail to add the proper back links, they can love you and leave you very quickly. Video sites have a very short lifespan on the first page; therefore use this opportunity to strengthen them with your back link strategy.

Once you have added back links to both video sites, I want you to turn your attention to your article and press release sites currently appearing on your first page.

> *Even if a site has landed on the second page of Google I ask that you also include the site into your back linking strategy.*

I have had sites come from as far back as page 5 to land on the first page because of proper back linking.

Like I said before, it is very important that you actively use your social networking sites because, the more active you are the higher your profile site will climb within your search results. You can also use Pingfm.com to save time with the updating process. Pingfm.com can update your twitter, Facebook, BLOG TALK RADIO, and Google Buzz accounts all at the same time.

Placing back links on the URL's of your indexed press releases aid those sites in remaining relevant within your search results.

Once you begin to understand and embrace the process of back linking, you will notice that all of your sites will increase in page rank and visibility. I have listed a few sources for building credible back links, but if you search the web you will find an array of ways to add back links to your sites.

Please keep in mind that only links relevant to your site will carry the weight required to lock a site firmly on page one. There are some who will try to skip to the front of the line by purchasing bulk orders of back links. This practice is considered to be a "Black Hat Strategy" by Google and will get you slapped.

The Google slap is similar to being placed in time out. Your site could run the risk of being removed permanently from Google's search results.

I advise you to stick to the recommended strategies for building back links that will guarantee that your sites never run the risk of getting banned by Google.

Complaint sites like the Rip-Off Report no longer carry the same venomous bite they once had, and this is due in part to the fact that Google has recently downgraded their page rankings.

At one-time if someone placed you in the Rip-Off Report that link would have been immediately placed at the top of the page. Recently I'm noticing that the Rip-Off Report is appearing towards the bottom of search results.

This is wonderful news for you if you are battling a site like Rip-Off Report. I still ask that you take the threat of the complaint site very seriously and aggressively follow the strategies that I have outlined for you in this section.

I recommended that you continue to attack your complaint site until it has landed on page six of your search results, only then will we declare you the winner.

CHAPTER 16

How to Defeat an Aggressive Attacker

> **Jab = Articles & Press Releases**
> **Uppercut = BLOG TALK RADIO Blogs**
> **Body Blows = Adding Backlinks**

Aggressive attackers are aggressive for a reason; they are motivated by negative emotions. In the past I have battled attacks from aggressive attackers, and there was always a great deal of emotions involved.

Aggressive attackers are determined to embarrass you in any way possible, as a result the first wave of the attack is often very brutal.

I can recall a recent client who shared with me a very heart wrenching story about a relationship that ended on a very sour note. My client had no idea that ending a 12-month relationship would cost him 24-months of humiliation resulting from negative blogs posted by his former lover. Even I was taken aback by the nature of this attack, it was very personal.

And this is the case normally whenever a former lover has decided to vent their hurt and pain on blogs and forums, but the depth of these attacks were definitely a first for me.

I have a firm policy of never judging any of the clients we take on because it could affect my motivation to help them. In many ways I take on the likeness of a defense attorney who has to defend the client regardless of their personal views. Even with that mindset there was still no way of escaping the fact my client had seriously smashed this woman's heart.

The reason I had to take into consideration my clients actions was because I have to anticipate her next move. At this point I'm fully aware that she is motivated by pain, and I now have to deal with a jilted lover.

Negative posts published by jilted lovers are far worse than those of disgruntled customers.

In cases where the negative post came from a disgruntled customer, they believed in their mind that they were doing a public service by publishing the details of their transaction.

A disgruntled customer has a tendency to run out of gas after a 45 day period, but this is rarely the case when dealing with a scorned lover.

Because their motivation is different, their publishing patterns are also very different and unpredictable.

Whereas a disgruntled customer would go to a site like complaints board, a jilted lover may create several sites to broadcast their pain.

In this section I wanted to highlight the worse-case scenario first because everything other than a jilted lover would be less excruciating to deal with. If your negative attacker is motivated by emotion then you can expect this attack to last for long period of time.

The reason is simple, every time something reminds them of you the process will start all over again.

In some cases it may take the person two years to bring their emotions under control, as in the case with my client. For 24 consecutive months his former lover posted negative information on a weekly basis without a pause, break, nor vacation from her relentless attack.

At first, I considered declining the client just based on the sheer amount of work that was going to be involved, and at first glance his first page appeared horrible.

Never wanting to back away from a challenge, I asked the client to give me the weekend to determine an estimate.

Once I had the opportunity to review each link posted on the first page, I determined that despite the larger number of embarrassing sites, none of them really carried any major weight. I then begin the process of checking the back links on each of the negative items and to my surprise none of the sites had any back links. I also conducted an Alexa rank search to determine the traffic rankings of the negative sites, and to my surprise again none of the sites had a page ranking.

This is very common whenever you're dealing with a large quantity of negative items, it doesn't necessarily mean that all of those sites are well put together. A well-designed attack would include a negative site that has over 80 relevant back links, which would make for a very difficult fight.

One of the characteristics of an emotional attack is sporadic postings.

Taking into consideration that there will be no method to this madness I had to devise a plan that would prevent future attacks no matter the nature, or frequency. Online attackers are very similar to terrorists in the method of their attacks.

The goal of terrorists is to cause as much damage as they can and then watch the destruction. This is also the case with online attackers; quite often they will take a moment just to appreciate the visibility of their negative attacks.

As we approach the strategy on how to defeat a negative attacker I first wanted you to understand the mindset and mentality of this form of attack. When dealing with negative post that are extremely personal, there has to be an enormous amount of time spent building a fence around the first page of your search results.

Here is the reality, the aggressive attacker will not simply go away our fade to black, they often return with a vengeance. So the main strategy in defeating a negative attacker is to fortify your defenses.

The sites that you have landed on the first page of your search results have to be so well constructed that they refuse to move regardless of any new published content.

By now we have already accepted that no one can delete a negative site from Google other than the host of the site; however, we do have the right to out publish our aggressive attackers. We simply have to out work them, to defeat them.

Jab = Articles & Press Release

The jabs that I want you to use against this particular opponent will be slightly different in design than the jabs that we have used previously. Because we are dealing with a very aggressive attacker who has publicly humiliated you online, I want you to publish content that gives insight to the beautiful person you really are.

Our goal is to use articles to present a more positive online image. How we plan to accomplish this is with a series of articles about your interests, volunteer efforts, community involvement, or any wonderful aspect of your personality. This is also accomplished with the use of multiple Q & A interviews, and profile sites that include sound files or videos.

And before you begin to frown on this technique please keep in mind that celebrities used this strategy all the time. In fact, any time a celebrity is are trying to promote their latest movie, book deal, or foundation one of the main things they will do is allow the media to have more access to their personal lives. Believe it or not the same technique will work perfectly for you.

The art of controlling public perception is to first embrace the following principle, "In life people will treat you as well as they perceive you, you have to control that perception."

Up until this point the only thing that was published about you came from someone who really disliked you.

There is nothing we can do about their personal feelings toward you; they have the right to feel that way.

You also have a right to offset the damage caused by the attack on your online reputation, which includes the right to shape public opinion.

Like I said before, no one has exclusive rights to the first page of Google. So let us introduce a more beautiful, realistic, and accurate image of you to the world.

Uppercut = BLOG TALK RADIO Blogs

Creating blogs will become extremely important to our efforts in repairing the damage caused by an aggressive attacker. We will use our blogs as a publishing tool in which we will begin to flood the Internet with positive content about the person you really are today.

In this chapter I have spent a considerable amount of time setting the stage for this technique from the angle of a personal attack, but this strategy will work the same even if your business has been attacked.

Our blogs are considered an uppercut because it is not a defensive move, but rather at an offensive attack.

With our blogs we will go on the offensive against the person who posted all of the horrible forum comments, by not acknowledging them at all. Instead we will talk about our areas of interest, our philosophies, current events, or simply create a "How To" blog.

Your blogs present the opportunity for you to give the world some insight to your personality and character. Blogs can be whatever you want them to be therefore you should always keep your blog free of dirty laundry.

Use your blogs to portray a positive image free from counterattacks or cat fights. You should never use your blogs to launch a personal attack nor should you use them to explain why you're being attacked. In doing so your will only sensationalize the attack and feed the ego of your attacker.

There was a very clear example of this strategy in a documentary about Coca-Cola that aired on MSNBC. During the documentary the interviewer noticed that none of the executives from Coca-Cola would ever even acknowledge their major competitor Pepsi.

In fact, they were so deliberate as to not even mention the name of their competitor in a sentence.

I remember watching the reporter arrive at this realization and thinking to myself that this is the perfect strategy to remain focused on your goals and the success of your brand.

My advice to you is to learn from the example of Coca-Cola and refrain from using your attackers name in any way, shape, form, or fashion. Instead we will focus on you and all of the positive attributes that you possess because this is truly the only way to offset a negative comment.

Not only will we keep our blog post positive, but we will also remain disciplined in our updating schedule. It is very important that you constantly update your blogs with unique and relevant content that is completely saturated with your keyword (your name or business name).

By now you're fully aware that Google loves content, especially unique and relevant content.

As long as content continues to be king of the Internet, you must supply Google with non-stop positive content about you or your business.

Our uppercut is our opportunity to strike back with a very preemptive, but yet positive response to your aggressive attacker.

Body Blows = Adding Backlinks

The entire purpose for creating all of this positive content is to land that content on the first page of Google. All of our jabs and uppercuts are designed to set up one major punch, the body blow.

We've already identified and that we are now dealing with a very emotional and aggressive attacker, therefore we can expect that this person will remain active for at least another year.

Now that we understand the motivations and mindset of our attacker we must now defend ourselves in a way that will make their attacks irrelevant.

If our aggressive attacker is constantly publishing websites and blogs but all of their material is landing on 5, 6, and 7, then you have just rendered them irrelevant.

By distributing your articles with the use of article directories and including the URL's of your blogs within the articles, you will begin the process of building strong relevant back links. You also should consider adding back links to the articles by embedding the targeted links within the new articles you're submitting.

The goal of the back links strategy is to firmly lock in all of the positive sites that you have created. Once we have locked in all of our positive sites, then it will not matter how many attacks are launched by our opponent. We fully understand that their efforts may continue for many months to come, but if none of their sites land on the first page of Google then chances are no one will notice it.

Use your body blows as often as possible to take control of your fight. This punch is not only highly effective but also a sure way to prevent future attacks. I challenge you to stay positive and not fan the flames by responding to anything posted about you or your business. Remember our lesson from the executives at Coca-Cola, only comment on you and your brand.

CHAPTER 17

How to Protect Your Business from Online Slander

> ### Jab = Articles and Press Releases

The Art of Creating your Own Public Relations Department

I have a client who is in the commercial lending field and recently he contacted me because his business was getting torched on a forum site. The site where the entire negative attack took place was a forum for mortgage and commercials brokers, need I say more.

I am not sure of all of the details of how commercial lending works but apparently there is this really dirty word in that industry called "Due Diligence Fees."

According to my client, there are fees associated with the discovery process for large funding requests in excess of two million dollars. The problem comes in when the person seeking the loan is denied by the funding source and the fees are non-refundable.

After a few people are denied a loan and the fees are not returned, I can understand how this could lead to a few of them feeling betrayed. Normally I would side with the group seeking the funding if it wasn't for the fact that they were told up front that the Due Diligence Fee is not a guarantee that their loan would get funded.

So out of the twenty-five loans that was funded during this period, the four that were declined (as a result of the feasibility study) posted comments claiming that they were scammed.

I hate scams just as much as the next person, but if you have received full disclosure and you still decided to enter into it willingly, then you can't claim that you were scammed. A scam is when I pay you to fix my car and you totally disappear off the face of the earth with my money, that qualifies as a scam.

The word scam has now replaced the act of taking full responsibility for your own losses. So instead of the investor admitting that they bet hard earned money on a long shot, they rather race to the victim category.

Scenarios like the one that I have just described takes place every day and is now the preferred method of conflict resolution.

The problem with this type of conflict resolution is that the issue never really gets addressed because both parties involved are now in attack mode.

As an advocate for business owners, I am very concerned about this trend of false accusations against legitimate businesses. The most frustrating part of all is that there isn't a board to protect a business from a false claims posted by a disgruntled customer.

This is why whenever I am asked to speak to business owners the first point that I emphasize is the need for every business owner (regardless of the size of the business) to develop their own public relations department.

As a business owner you can delegate one member of your staff to assist you in monitoring the online reputation of your business. The best part of it all is that there is no equipment to purchase; everything that you need to set up your own PR department already exists within your current office.

How to Fight Back!

As a business owner you have the right to defend yourself against online attacks from both disgruntled customers as well as competitors.

Your brand took years to build and sits as a symbol of your life's work. Listed on the following pages are two things that you can do today that will begin the process of building a fence around your brand.

Jab = Articles and Press Releases

Become your own publicist - You have a right to publish positive content about your business, exercise this right! Remember what I said earlier, Google remains on the sidelines of this big mess that they have created by referring to all published content as "3rd Party Submissions," therefore you need to get your own 3rd party to defend your company.

You can accomplish this without spending all of your profits, especially with the help of Social Media Sites.

At least twice a month your PR department should send out a press release announcing positive news about your business or services.

If you take an active role in publicizing the accomplishments of your business and include testimonials from happy customers, you will begin the process of securing your online reputation.

Here is the risk of not taking my advice and doing nothing at all; whatever was posted on the negative site about your business and will begin to define your business.

Once a disgruntled customer has posted negative comments about your business, those items will remain index by Google forever.

Despite that negative comments are indexed forever, it doesn't mean that they have to remain visible forever on your first page.

By actively publishing positive content about your business you are taking a proactive approach by securing and competing for all available spaces on the first page of your search results.

Just as the Golden rule of real estate stresses the importance of "location, location, location" this rule also holds true when fighting for available locations in Google.

Landing in Google News

Even as a small business owner, there are tools available to you that will help you land your stories on major news wires. I want you to take this opportunity to become familiar with how to prepare a press release about your business.

I have included a few pointers in the fight training section of this book on press release preparation; however I ask that you take a few moments to practice how to prepare a search engine optimized press release.

Despite the lengthy name, the concept is actually very simple. A search engine optimized press release means that the name of your business is strategically placed throughout the press release to improve search engine indexing.

The major press release sites will require that your press release is newsworthy and original content.

The number one way to make sure that all of your press releases are accepted by the major sites is to write them as if a reporter is doing a story about your business.

A press release site that I absolutely love is Online PR News.

This site has an unbelievable press release distribution service that will not only distribute your press release to other PR sites but will also submit your press release to Google News.

The more you submit positive press about your business, the more you will begin to re-establish yourself as a reputable business.

Generating a constant flow of positive press can also position you as an industry leader in your field. Once your press release submissions begin to land in Google News those items will remain searchable permanently.

Another benefit to landing your press release in Google News is Google will actually post a link on the first page of your search results leading directly to your press release.

I suggest that you keep your press release submissions between 300 - 500 words; anything longer runs the risk of being considered an article.

Please remember to include your Web address at the bottom of each press release, in doing so you will create solid back links to your website.

To create your own public relations department within your small business means you will have to control the information visible about you or your brand.

The more content you publish, the more you will begin to establish your brand as a preferred choice for potential customers.

Another benefit to publishing your own press release is that many of your submissions will land under keywords constantly being searched by your customers.

To accelerate the learning curve I have dedicated an entire chapter to explaining how to use a press release to drive traffic to your website, and increase sales.

Protecting your online reputation and brand promotion are two extremely effective techniques to use in your fight against online slander.

The main goal of this chapter is to empower you to take control, and to simplify the process required to protect you and your business from online slander.

I ask that you take any online attack against your business very serious because it has the potential to become cancerous.

The good news is, if you've followed the steps that I have outlined in this book you will have the theory and develop the practical skills required to remove any potentially damaging remarks out of view of your clientele.

I encourage you to defend your brand as vigorously as major corporations defend their brands.

What it all comes down to is money; negative online articles can put you out of business within 90 days.

The defense of your brand is a fight that you must take very personal because it is also an attack on your livelihood. You must successfully defend your brand from all forms of Internet slander to remain competitive within your field. Not only are your sales depending on it, but your legacy is depending on it as well.

CHAPTER 18

Negative Information Regarding Court Cases and Convictions

> **Hook = Video Marketing**
> **Straight Right = Created Domains**
> **Uppercut = BLOG TALK RADIO Blogs & Profiles**
> **Body Blows = Adding Backlinks**

I have to be honest with you; the toughest fight I have ever encountered was trying to remove a court published PDF from the first page of Google.

This particular PDF was unlike any PDF I've ever faced because of the way it was published.

I admit that it is very difficult to go against a site that has been constructed by someone who knows just as much as I do about search engine optimization.

Nevertheless, I accepted the job and I gave my client my word that I would give it my best effort.

After only 72 hours into the job I wanted to send the customer all of his money back when a note saying "I'm sorry I even accepted this job."

This is what it's like to be in the field of reputation management, it means you're fighting monsters every day. I have never been one to criticize another company for the amount of money they charge clients to remove negative items from the first page of Google because I know firsthand how much work is involved. All it takes is one site from hell like the one I just described and all of your John Madden Football time is gone.

It's becoming common practice for the clerk of courts to publish verdict results on their websites. The only problem with this practice is the moment it's published the content can also be indexed by Google. Once a site is indexed by Google chances are it will land in the number one spot under your name.

Usually when I encounter a PDF website there are only a few subpages connected to that URL, but with this site there were a total of nine published pages resulting from this trial. This is one of those moments when you ask yourself what in hell were you thinking when you accepted this job?

Despite the fact that this was one of my toughest jobs ever, I also credit this enormous challenge with teaching me some very powerful strategies.

Why PDF's Rank So High in Google

PDF's are pure documents. What I mean by this is someone uploaded the document to the Internet.

We all know that Google has an insatiable appetite for content and PDF's represent the purest form of content.

Not only that, a PDF typically represents information without any form of monetized advertising.

Over the years Google has become the preferred site for advertisers. Whenever possible Google will make every attempt to provide searchers with relevant content within their organic search results.

If you have searched your name and have discovered that the clerk of court has uploaded the entire judgment of the court onto their website, then you may want to do a few push-ups before we proceed.

Another challenge of dealing with a PDF site is that the URL normally ends with (.Gov). Here is where the Battle for Middle Earth begins; you're going up against a domain that Google ranks as high as any other URL in the world.

Education (. EDU), and Government (. Gov) domains can present an enormous challenge if you're trying to move one of these sites off the first page of Google.

The reason these two sites are more difficult than others to remove off the first page is because Google believes that the content on both sites are not only relevant to the keyword but also has no commercial value.

In a recent conversation with one of my colleagues, he was updating me on a theory that he has been studying over the past nine months. If you've ever had someone present you with a theory that you hoped was dead wrong, well this was one of them.

My buddy had arrived at the theory that Google was beginning to incorporate the idea of diversity within their search results.

To simplify this, what he was getting at was Google includes both negative and positive search results to create balance.

I am not sure where he got this information from being that the employees of Google are sworn to life or death secrecy, but he was very confident in his beliefs.

As our debate shifted back and forth, I explained to him that I battle negative sites every day and have seen no proof of this theory with the exception of PDF sites.

Now the reason why I wanted to share that story with you was to prepare you for the effort it's going to take to remove that PDF site off the first page of Google. Can it be done? Yes it can. Will it take a lot of work? Yes it will.

Having said that, you're left with no other choice other than to take on the task yourself or pay someone to do it for you.

In any case the site will have to be removed or it will continue to provide the public with every intricate detail of your personal life.

Since I am giving you the gloom & doom of dealing with a PDF site please allow me to present you with some good news.

I have been successful in removing PDF sites from the first page of Google more times than I can even count. Now when I come face-to-face with a PDF site from a court related trial I instantly began my automation process.

My automation process consists of a punch strategy that has given him me the greatest success rate when dealing with court related documents in the form of a PDF.

Listed below you will find my punch combinations that will help you defeat court related PDF sites as well as (.Gov) domains.

Hook= Video Marketing

Whenever I take on a PDF site my first goal is to land a few very hard punches as quickly as I can. In the world boxing this series of rapid punches is referred to as a "Mix." The first wave of my mixed punch combination requires that I upload multiple videos with the help of video sites like the Daily Motion and Meta Café.com.

The reason I want you to begin this punch strategy with these two sites is because of their sheer speed at landing on the first page of Google. PDF sites typically only have a small number of back links therefore any resistance we get will not be because the site has a high popularity rating. All of our resistance will come from the Google Bot, who has been programmed to identify relevant content.

Here is the advantage of using video marketing; the technology is relatively new, that means the Google bot will perceive that the videos are more relevant.

As I mentioned before video sites can have a very short lifespan on the first page, especially if you only upload one. You will have more success with landing your videos permanently on the first page of Google if you upload multiple videos.

Once you upload multiple videos, Google will eventually grab two of your videos and index them permanently on the first page of your search results. I have had students of this course voice privacy concerns about posting videos of themselves on sites like YouTube.

To remedy these concerns I suggest that you convert a PowerPoint video (search PPT to video) into a video file that can be uploaded onto Tube sites. For this purpose I want to recommend a product called Moyea (www.moyea.com) Moyea PPT to Video Converter.

With this software you can basically create a video from any PowerPoint presentation and uploaded it to Daily Motion and Meta-Café.com instantly.

Imagine the power of being able to create a positive video presentation about you or your business and have it land permanently on the first page of your search results. This is the power you will have with this strategy.

Straight Right = Created Domains

In my experience Google will index a website that has the keyword within the domain name higher than a PDF site. To increase the effectiveness of your straight right punch you will have to create a website search engine optimized with your keyword (your name or the name of your business).

If your business already has a website then this is a good opportunity to register multiple domains and have them pointed toward your current website. If you had a web designer to build your website then recruit him into your efforts to land your new domains on your first page.

It is definitely a good idea to construct three unique websites, all with relevant content and a custom domain name. This strategy comes straight out of my playbook when it comes to removing the negative site off the first page of Google.

My goal is to land sites on the first page of Google that will not move regardless of any future attacks. The major benefits of using this strategy is that the custom domains will out rank the court site for placement in your search results.

There is really no way around it, if you're trying to remove a stubborn site off the first page of Google then it will take more relevant sites in order to accomplish that goal.

To simplify this process I always use Intuit Web Designs (www.intuit.com) because of their easy to use templates. Intuit has templates that are basically cut & paste ready which helps me build really nice sites in no time.

To add additional power to your created sites, I highly recommend that you include a RSS News Feed to each page of your custom designed website. Sites that have RSS news feeds are constantly updated which means that Google will increase your page rank every time they crawl the site.

Uppercut = BLOG TALK RADIO Blogs & Profiles

The uppercut falls directly in line with the other punches in your punch strategy. With the help of social networking profiles from Twitter and Facebook you will have the opportunity to land two additional 1st page placements in Google.

I never really embraced Twitter as an ideal social networking site, but I absolutely love that their profiles typically land on the first page of Google.

The more you interact with Twitter the higher your profile listing will climb in Google's page rankings. I suggest that you send tweets at least twice a week to maintain an active posting schedule on Twitter. It is always a good idea to tweet your most recent press release, articles, and blog posts because in doing so it creates additional back links to your website.

Never under estimate the power of social networking profiles to land on the first page of Google. Every month a new social networking site cracks the top 50 top rated sites in the world according to Alexa ranking systems.

I am always on the lookout for the next Facebook because Google is also on the lookout for the next Facebook. If you simply follow the herds then you will continuously stay up-to-date with the latest top rated social networking sites with the potential to dominate the first page of Google.

You Have to Build It

The way to remove personal information from a court trial is to land solid sites on the first page of Google that will remain there permanently. Just a little bit of effort right now will pay off in the long run.

The peace of mind of knowing that court papers regarding your felony conviction will not return to the first page of Google is priceless.

I also want you to consider Word Press blogs as well as Blog Talk Radio in your strategy to land permanent sites on the first page.

Personally I am not that familiar with Word Press blog in terms of building these really elaborate sites, but I can attest first hand to their ability to land on the 1st page of Google.

I encourage you to incorporate both blogging platforms into your punch strategy because both sites have a proven recorded of ranking high in Google.

CHAPTER 19

How Bounce Back From Negative Publicity and Bad Press

The Art of Making a Comeback

As I watched the Lakers win another NBA Championship what really stood out to me was not Kobe Bryant's dynamic performance, but rather the success of his public relations team.

It was not so long ago that he was caught in a world wind of controversy that now seems like a distant memory.

Some celebrities can bounce back from career ending screw up's, and some just simply fade to black in disgrace as their career comes to an end.

Take for example Mel Gibson's latest PR disaster in which he warns his girlfriend that she could get raped by a "Pack of Ni***ers." We can definitely put a fork in Mr. Gibson, because he is now officially done in Hollywood.

Mel Gibson's latest racial rant has once again landed him on the front page of every entertainment publication around the world and was the lead story on Entertainment Tonight (ET).

Even the best of my PR colleagues are telling me that they will send Mel Gibson's call straight to voice mail if he calls them seeking damage control with this one.

Please keep in mind that fans have already forgiven him once for his first cacophony of defamatory comments about the Jewish Community.

Now we can only wonder which ethnic group he will attack next in his latest epic "Mel Gibson's March to the Sea."

Cases like Mel Gibson's are the extreme end when it comes to dealing with negative publicity. You can take some comfort in knowing that there is hope for you, if your latest screw up is north of Mel Gibson's.

Unlike Gibson, Kobe Bryant did the "Right Thing" with our forgiveness and proved that his incident was a mistake in judgment.

As a culture we can understand a stupid mistake, if your actions afterwards totally contradict the reason you had to call an "I'm so sorry" press conference.

Ray Lewis, Hugh Grant, Winona Ryder, Randy Moss, Eddie Murphy, Jimmy Swaggart, Justin Timberlake, and Todd Bridges just to name a few, all have done extraordinary jobs at recovering from potentially career ending mistakes.

How to Move Forward From a Nightmare

Kobe Bryant up to this point has lived an exceptional life since he made is public mistake, and because of that he has honored our forgiveness.

After Magic Johnson's Press Conference on November 7, 1991, we have never read another negative article about his lifestyle.

It's not the fall that gets you banned from public view; it's the repeated falls that causes us to wipe our hands of you. Now the same rules that apply to famous athletes and celebrities also applies to you.

The first step in moving forward from bad publicity is to never make that mistake again.

It's not as important that you convince the public that you made the biggest mistake of your life, but rather your ability to convince yourself that it was simply stupid and out of character.

Listed below are three tips that will help you change public perception after your own personal press conference of shame.

- **Don't Ever Do It Again** - I know this may seem very obvious to those of you who possess common sense, but as my grandmother would always say "common sense is not common."

If you ever think about repeating the same mistake just remember the example of Kobe Bryant and Mel Gibson.

- **Change your lifestyle** - Get control of your habits, and even consider new friends if the change will place you in the company of more responsible people.

At this point you have to take your personal life in a totally different direction. Try to search yourself in an attempt to find out what made you commit such a stupid act. Take responsibility for your actions and never, never ever, place the blame on a 3rd party.

- **Stay Out Of The Press** - After your press conference of shame, disappear from the press for a period of 1-3 years. You need to allow time for the smoke to settle, and time to pass before you're out generating new publicity. Even if you're involved in something positive, the perception of your participation will still cast a negative cloud. Avoid making charity appearances or making huge donations because the perception will be that you're trying to buy your way back into good grace. The best thing to do at this point is re-focus on your career or business in a way that adds value to your brand.

- **Reinvent Yourself** - You are the CEO of you. Every decision from this point has to place you in the best possible light, and the possible environment. You have to become the person you really are in the eyes of public perception.

  You have the right to totally reinvent your brand in a way that looks and feels genuine, without appearing fake. To reinvent doesn't mean to go over the top, but to simply bleach your image. You can accomplish this with a change in your wardrobe, public appearances, associations, mindset, attitude, expression, and ventures.

The best part about recovering from bad publicity is people will root for you because they really want to see you bounce back. Never forget that everyone loves the Comeback Kid.

Ray Lewis of the Baltimore Ravens went from the darkest days of his life, to one of the most respected and admired men on, and off the football field. I encourage you to learn from your mistake and change your life in a way that would make the likely hood of this ever happening again extremely unlikely.

CHAPTER 20

Vanity Search Your Name before Your Next Job Interview

Jab = Articles & Press Release
Uppercut = BLOG TALK RADIO Blog

If I were to search your name in Google right now, what would I find? The answer to this question is not as scary as the fact that most people are not aware of negative items that are appearing on the first page of their search results.

Having damaging or humiliating items on the 1st page of your search results will definitely make it very difficult to find a new gig and here is why.

In a recent poll a large percentage of Human Resource managers admitted to conducting a Vanity Search on prospective applicants in an attempt to gauge their character. In the same poll 85% of HR managers replied that they always accept the first page results as factual.

Image the implications of your bachelor party pictures from a recent trip to Vegas appearing on the first page of your search results.

Do you see where I'm going with this?

Why Should You Care

Sites like Google have become more than just website search engines; they have now become people search engines. Google has constructed dozens of large database centers throughout the United States, for no other reason than to fine tune search results.

The main purpose of these centers are to store all search results from that particular region, and link searchers to relevant content from that area of the country.

Google is very secretive about the locations and functions of these databases nevertheless here is the part most relevant to you.

If I am in your town and I search your name in a Google search bar, then chances are your name will appear at the top of the search results.

The best case scenario is to search your name and nothing appears, but even that is wishful thinking due to sites like Facebook and Twitter. Somewhere along the way we have lost all of our common sense when it comes to social networking sites.

Sure in the beginning it was great to catch up with old friends from high school, but the side effects have resulted in private Tweets now appearing on the first page of Google. Yikes!

Once a tweet has landed on the 1st page of Google, it will remain indexed forever. If you're counting on the negative items to evaporate then you're in for a rude awakening.

Quite often negative sites appearing under your name are not as innocent as a tweet from your girlfriend; unfortunately most negative items were placed there intentionally, and deliberately.

> *Just because a negative site is appearing on the first page of your search results doesn't mean that it has a right to be there.*

Remember what I said earlier, your name is your brand and just as large corporations vigorously protect their brands so should you.

Update Your Resume and your Search Results

As you prepare your resume I also suggest that you search your name in search engines. Nothing is worse than to miss out on the opportunity of a lifetime all because the interviewer discovered an old online article from back when you were freshmen in college. Maybe you have already gone on several interviews and now coming to the realization that no one has called you back despite your experience and college degrees.

Conducting a vanity search with your name as the keyword will allow you to see what a potential employer will see the moment they search your name.

Are You Still Unemployed? You Probably Should Search Your Name in Google

You may think it's something small or insignificant, but that incident that made the county newspaper back in 1998 may be the reason you're still unemployed.

With an increase in unique users, sites like Facebook and Twitter are primarily responsible for more and more personal information finding its way to the Internet.

Now, if a HR manager wanted to dig deeper into your character you can bet the farm that they will turn to Google for a full report of who you really are.

Not only are new hires finding it difficult to find a job with humiliating content appearing in their search results, but even tenured employees are now losing their jobs as a result of something that was posted on their Facebook wall.

This was basically unheard of five years ago but with SMO (Social Media Optimization) now dominating search engines, the result has led to many corporations updating their policies and procedures manuals to include end of shift conduct rules.

Facebook Firings are adding new members to list of the unemployed every day.

There are some days when our phones ring off the hook from people seeking help on how to remove either a picture or personal information now appearing online.

These types of calls are always extremely urgent because the client is trying to remove the content before their supervisors discover it.

This problem has become epidemic in its damage to the reputations of many of the people that seek our help as well as a total violation of their privacy.

The best thing that you can do to protect yourself from having personal information find its way to the 1st page of Google is to block your friends on Facebook from posting personal information your wall.

Many of the damaging posts are placed there by friends just reminiscing on events from when they were teens or as a joke and that wall post gets indexed by Google.

Once Google has indexed a comment from Facebook or Twitter, they will not take it down. Google is considered to an online archive, therefore under law they are not responsible/libel for any comments published by a 3rd party.

In the case of your personal information now appearing on the 1st page of your search results, your buddy is actually the 3rd party.

Three tips for preventing your personal information from getting indexed by Google:

1. Stay away from Blogs and Forums - Google loves blogs and forums because of their ability to generate original content for readers. The only problem is if you post anything about you or your family then those comments will rank really high in your search results.

2. Never post pictures from a night on the town - This has to be the quickest way to get fired or definitely get you the dreadful meeting from senior supervisors. Pictures will even get indexed above website content placing them at the top of your

search results, so please avoid posting pictures of you and your friends.

3. Don't Tweet Your Life - Try to avoid posting any private information in the form of a tweet. Tweets will get indexed with the comment in quotes, and placed on the 1st page of Google. Facebook and Twitter are ranked very high in Alexa's System; therefore anything posted in a social networking site has a very strong possibility of landing on the 1st page of your search results.

The best advice is probably the same advice your Dad would give you, and that is to keep your personal life separate from the Internet.

No one should have the ability to type your name in a search engine and find out your favorite books, restaurant, or even the details of your new relationship. Let's return back to common sense people!

If you recently had an interview and everything went well but they never called him you back, then chances are you may have damaging online content appearing under your name in Google.

In the same poll of HR managers a very large percentage of them admit that they start their background checks with a Google search of the applicant's name, and if all checks out only then will they pay for a police report.

The Power of a Professionally Polished E-Profile

It is almost impossible to view an evening news broadcast without hearing about unemployment reports and the lack of private sector jobs.

Our nation is in a tug of war in priorities when it comes to which is more important, Healthcare Reform or Unemployment.

All you really have to do is survey any unemployed professional and they will quickly help you decide which one is more important, a cure for high unemployment. Scores and scores of unemployed degreed professionals are now excepting the reality that this is perhaps the most competitive job market our nation has experienced since the end of World War II.

Back in the early 90's, just your degree from Southern University was enough to land you in a really nice position with just about any corporation across the country. This current job market is so competitive that you will need your Bachelors, and even possibly a Master's Degree from Tulane University to really stand out.

With the current unemployment rate resting soundly at 9.3% as of May 2010, there will have to be something exceptionally unique about your resume or profile to catch the attention of overwhelmed human resource professionals.

The Internet to the Rescue

E-Profiles have really started to catch on over the past six months for the ability to help degreed professionals highlight their credentials.

E-Profiles are webpage's created for the purpose of promoting an applicant's positives, and relevance to the available position. Think of it as creating your own perfect image or even better becoming your own publicist.

This latest Internet craze has given rise to a new "Internet-dustry "called E-Profile Web Services.

E- Profile Web Services deliver an attractive digital snapshot of you or your business in a webpage format that clients and agencies can access instantly via your secure personal E-Profile address.

More and more people are turning to the Internet to compete for available customers and employment opportunities.

Not so long ago, a simple resume was all you needed to get your foot in the door, today you really have to work hard at promoting your credentials.

An E-Profile places your content directly in front of the decision maker in a way the presents you in the best possible light.

Another positive to incorporating an E-Profile with your resume is that you can also add a professional video presentation as well as additional pages dedicated to your work experience.

If you are going to compete for the limited amount of opportunities offered by the current job market then your resume and content will have to compete against more savvy applicants.

The good news for those that manage to stand out from the crowd will be that initial call from HR to schedule an interview.

Applicants who fail to separate themselves from the masses will get left behind to battle it out for the less desirable positions.

Jab = Articles & Press Release

Uppercut = BLOG TALK RADIO Blog

It is very important that your first page search results work for you rather than against you if you're in the market for a better paying job.

Creating a series of articles about you or your profession is a great way to not only control the information visible on the first page, but also give your potential employer a glimpse of your writing style.

If you are unemployed then this is a great opportunity to begin to publish content relevant to your field or the position that you're applying for.

At this point I'm confident that your potential employer will search your name in Google, therefore we will do everything possible to shape their opinion or you.

A press release about one of your recent accomplishments is a great way to add credibility to your resume.

There is really no need to stretch the truth in reference to your previous experience, include in your press release a verifiable accomplishment from your resume.

Blogging about topics relevant to your field is also a great way of demonstrating your depth, and level of experience.

CHAPTER 21

How to Create Positive Publicity

> **Jab = Articles & Press Release**
> **Hook= Video Marketing**
> **Straight Right = Created Domains**
> **Uppercut = BLOG TALK RADIO Blogs**
> **Body Blows = Adding Backlinks**

This entire book has been dedicated to the removal of negative content from the first page of Google. With this last and final round I want to discuss how to improve your online reputation by creating positive publicity.

The interesting thing about creating positive publicity is that you will utilize the same strategies, but this time with less focus on the negative items.

Once we have removed all of the negative content from the first page of Google, all that should remain are positive sites. Every item within our punch combination was designed to improve your online image, and enhance your profile.

Having a cloud of negative publicity hanging over your head can make it very difficult to accomplish many of your goals in life.

So much of our lives are connected to the Internet that it grieves me to admit that the Internet can play a major role in shaping your overall perception.

Positive Publicity Has To Be Earned

The more effort you put in to improving your online reputation, the more it will pay off for you in either opportunities or sales.

Positive publicity is a gift that keeps on giving the more you invest in self-promotion. Sometimes self-promotion serves as the ignition switch that causes others to notice you.

Going forward you must develop the ability to promote yourself or your business in ways that attracts positive press.

In the chapters of this book I have covered several SEO strategies that are highly effective in removing negative content and also equally effective in depositing positive content onto the first page of Google.

So for the remainder of this book I want to recap how each punch strategy can promote your positives as well as drive sales traffic to your website.

Jab = Articles & Press Release

Before I discovered article marketing I was spending a ton of money on Google AdWords.

Unlike Google AdWords, which have now become famous for click fraud, traffic derived from article marketing has proven to be very profitable.

There are articles that I published to promote my business over a year ago that are still sending traffic to my website today. As a matter of fact I have an article titled *"How To Delete Negative Search Results About You In Google"* that has provided me with more sales than any other form of paid advertising.

This one article has sent me about 67 sales, and the best part is I am not paying anything for those leads.

This is the power of article marketing, you submit it one time and it remains out there forever. The general theme of this book was based on how to get Google to work for you rather than against you, and article marketing is just another example of this principle.

Article marketing gives you the power to land on any page of Google you choose because it levels the playing field.

There will be times when it will be next to impossible to get your website to land under very competitive keyword, but your article will simply slip in at the top of the page. Like with everything there are exceptions, there are a few keywords that no one has been able to penetrate.

With a little creative persistence you can have the same success I have had in landing my articles under very lucrative keywords.

Here is the Secret

Title your article the exact name of the page you're trying to land on. It's not complicated, so please don't complicate it.

> *The title of your article will determine where it gets indexed in Google, not the tags.*

I know much emphasis has been placed on the tags, but the tags have to work in conjunction with the title. The title as a standalone will get indexed regardless of the presence of tags, trust me because I have tested the theory.

The Gift That Keeps Giving

My articles are my pride and joy, and I value many of them just as much as I value my website. Whenever I receive a visitor to my website that came from one of my articles, it's like receiving an endorsement from a random visitor.

Article marketing can be a very valuable tool as you move away from negative publicity to an area of notoriety and acceptance.

Another benefit to article marketing is its ability to establish you as an expert within your niche. The more Internet searchers begin to discover your name and your articles, the more they will begin to associate you as an industry professional.

As you move from negative publicity to positive, there has to be a renewed focus on brand development and promotion.

Article marketing is also a great way to display your knowledge of a given subject. Well prepared articles give readers the impression that you are providing them with valuable information without the bombardment of advertisements.

The ultimate goal is to drive unique traffic to your website, and hopefully convert that traffic into sales or leads.

Once one of your articles has been indexed by Google that article will remain in cyberspace forever.

Your articles are the equivalent of legions of salesmen dispersed throughout the web driving sales to your location, all at no additional cost to you.

To become an effective article marketer you must provide your readers with useful relevant content, without the big sales pitch.

Each article should end with one request that says "if you like to receive additional information then please visit my website." Extending an invitation to visit your website is far more effective than trying to force the readers to your site.

With the use of Articlebase, which happens to be my favorite article directory, you will gain a presence in areas that would have taken your website years to penetrate.

The Power of a Press Release

A well written press release is a great way to create positive publicity for you or your business and attract media attention. A press release still has the ability to land on major news wires, and send journalists directly to your website.

An effective press release is a great way to make an announcement about your product or service and it also provides you with an avenue to saturate the web with your positive publicity.

Once you write a press release and submit it to a mainstream distributor, other press release sites will also gain access to your positive news.

Most press release directories are connected to other news hubs, which will allow your story to very quickly spread around the world.

I can recall a time when one of my press release announcements was re-circulated on several news wires in Australia. At first I wasn't really sure of how so many people from this one particular region discovered my website until one of them informed me that they came across one of my press releases.

I really encourage you to master the art of announcing your exciting news. Learning how to promote your positives is a great way to keep your name in front of potential customers.

Customers gravitate toward people and companies that appear to be the leaders in their field. A press released story about your latest accomplishment is a great way to drive home the point that I am a leader of the pack.

One of the wonderful aspects of a press release submission has to be its ability to land on the first page of Google. A press release is considered newsworthy, and therefore given more credibility than traditional websites.

Getting your press release to land on the first page of Google requires the same strategy as getting your article to land on the first page of Google; your title has to be perfect.

I am always developing new and creative ways of including my keyword into the title of my press releases.

Getting indexed in Google is not as important as getting indexed on the pages where your customers are searching.

> *For a list of more creative ways to land your press release in targeted areas of Google, then please pick up a copy of our How to Fight Google and Win Workbook at www.removeslander.com.*

The Power of Saturation

To establish a presence on the Internet will require a great deal of diligence on your part. The Internet will reward those that actively publish their content on a continuous basis with the gift of visibility. Our main objective is to achieve complete visibility on just about every search engine on the Internet.

I know we have focused the majority of our energy on how to affect the search results within Google, but there are other search engines that can produce worthwhile results. Take for instance Yahoo, which is now currently ranked as the number two search engine in the world.

I have noticed that Google pays very close attention to the changes that take place in Yahoo therefore it may be a good strategy to target Yahoo first in an attempt to get Google to follow you.

Google will actively crawl sites that have been indexed by Yahoo, thus causing them to index the same site in their databases. Despite being ranked number three in the world, Bing also has the ability to get your content out to millions of people around the world.

Blog It

With the use of Word Press and Blog Talk Radio blogs you will have the opportunity to thoroughly saturate the Internet with positive content about you or your business. Blogs give you the opportunity to write about whatever you find interesting or newsworthy and also the ability to develop a membership base.

I ask that you use your blogs to crank out content on a continuous basis in an attempt to saturate the Internet with useful information about your name and brand.

Keep Building

Landing pages (commonly called micro sites) has become a great way to expand your reach around the Internet. Micro sites are one page websites designed to display either video or additional information from your website. The goal of a landing page is to drive unique traffic to your main site.

Our main website (www.removeslander.com) has about 14 additional landing pages throughout the Internet. The reason I've published so many additional single page websites is that it allows me to focus those pages on one particular aspect of my service.

Landing pages are not intended to be the final destination for your traffic, but more of a service road that leads searchers to your main highway.

I once had a customer tell me that no matter where he searched on the internet he would always find my site on the 1st page of Google. Of course this made me extremely proud because I had worked so hard to make sure that he would find me.

In this book I have given you every secret I have to not only remove a negative item from the first page of Google and how to use the Internet to promote your positive attributes.

Everything that I have outlined in this book will all work together to repair and rebuild your online reputation. Every milestone that I have achieved was accomplished using the exact same strategies embedded in each chapter of this book. If you commit yourself to applying these strategies then you too can expect to reap the rewards of your efforts.

The more you engage in article marketing, press release submission, blogging, website creation, and link building the more your website will increase in value.

Our primary focus has been on Google but the strategies in this book will work with any search engine on the web.

The sense of accomplishment you will enjoy from totally wiping your first page search results clean of any negative items will truly be a defining moment for you as a publisher. My goal with book was to take you from a lowly position of the victim, to an empowered realm of a conqueror.

From this point forward you are no longer a victim of Internet slander but rather an accomplished Internet publisher. As a publisher you now have full control over the entire Internet as it relates to the presentation of your online image.

As a publisher you now will dictate when, where, why, and how your brand will be presented to the world. As a publisher you will define your image and the content of your character, not your attacker.

Some in my industry have criticized me for revealing many of the techniques that I have shared with you in the pages of this book because it is the threat to their livelihoods. My position has always remained the same; a candle will never lose any of its illumination by lighting another candle.

Allow me to be the first to welcome you welcome to the fraternal order of Internet publishers.

CHAPTER 22

Become King of the Internet

Would you like to become King of the Internet? I think I have discovered the golden grail that will help you dominate the first page of Google for just about any keyword. I know you're probably saying to yourself "yea right" but the reason you discovered my book was because of my secret weapon, I-News Wire.

Ever since I stumbled upon I-News Wire (www.i-newswire.com) I have completely controlled the first page of Google. If you are trying to create positive publicity after going through a publicly humiliating ordeal then I suggest that you head over to their site and sign up, here's why.

Listed below is an actual compliment that I sent to the owner of I-News Wire, as you can tell I am also a happy client.

Subject: NO WAY!

YES WAY!!!

If I hadn't witnessed it with my own eyes, I would have never believed it, I had almost 1000 visitors in a 24 hour period. If you only knew the money I have wasted on Google AdWords. My wife checked our traffic history and informed me that we have never had that many unique visitors visit one of our sites. The press release on How to fight Google and win is a hit, now we have to figure out a way to convert more of those visitors into sales - LOL.

I just wanted to tell you how awesome and powerful your press releases really are, 48 hours later we are still on the first page of Google News. The money we are spending for your top plan is the best money we have spent on Internet marketing in two years. I have become a walking commercial for I-News Wire, enjoy your weekend.

Thank you

TJ

You have my permission to use this testimonial to promote your brand.

Tyronne Jacques

I-News Wire Press Releases will land in Google News within one hour after you hit submit (These results are based on my inclusion times. Individual results may vary.) for any keyword. If you are trying to promote yourself by creating positive publicity then it's time to start publishing press releases using I-News Wire.

I am not a paid spokesperson for their service, but I have an obligation to you to keep you abreast of what works best at minimal cost.

If you knew how much money I lost using Google AdWords only to have one press release posted by I-News Wire outperform 90 days of Google AdWords. Once you're in Google news, your positive information will remain under your name permanently, imagine that.

Imagine being able to create something positive about you and your business every day and the publishing power to make sure your brand is visible.

I am not saying that you have to select their top plan, but if you really want to flood the internet with positive content then I suggest their premium plan for a few months. Another benefit you will enjoy is a few of my press releases were picked up by other major publications like USA Today and CBS Market Watch, which are very powerful back links to have.

There are a few free sites that I have listed for your convenience but any money spent with I-News Wire is money well spent.

CONCLUSION

As a Public Relations Professional, I offer you the same advice that I mandate of my clients. When it comes to rebuilding your life, you will have to subscribe to the following principal or you risk having your name or brand banished and forever tarnished.

Philippians 4:8

Finally, brethren, whatsoever things are true, whatsoever things are honest, whatsoever things are just, whatsoever things are pure, whatsoever things are lovely, whatsoever things are of good report; if there be any virtue, and if there be any praise, think on these things

Thank you

Tyronne Jacques

tj@removeitnow.com

RESOURCES

Sample Article # 1

- Fired Because of Facebook by Tyronne Jacques

It seems almost mind blowing to think about it, but you can get fired for something you posted on Facebook. How did we arrive at this point? Did anyone see this coming? A report came out last week that said Facebook users now spend on average of 6 hours per week logged in. That's correct, 6 hours precious hours per week logged into a website!

Someone who has just hatched out of an egg shield would probably ask what in the hell are all of these people doing on a website for 6 hour? To answer your question Mr. Hatchling, posting personal information about themselves all over the web. Posting their whereabouts, their children's names, and even when they plan to leave for a 7 day cruise while having their address listed in their profiles. Yikes

Call it carried away or merely obsessed with staying connected, but somewhere we have lost our common sense when it comes to sites like Facebook, and Twitter.

So you have just gotten fired for something you posted on Facebook? Was it fair that they fire you for something that took place on your personal time? I would say no it's not fair, but is it legal? Absolutely it is.

A company has a right to protect its brand, and image. The people that represent their brand which includes you are expected to conduct themselves in a manner that is in line with the ethics of that company.

This is the reason that 93% of Human Resources Managers polled admitted to searching a potential employee's name in Google as a part of the hiring process.

Once you have posted potentially damaging content regarding your personal life on Facebook it will makes it way to your first page search results in Google within 10 days. Any and all personal pictures and comments posted to Google will get archived in their database forever!

In a recent interview with **(your name)** of the (your company) Work force Development Group he said that more and more employers are monitoring the online activities of their employee's.

"There once was a time when you clocked out a 5:00 pm and that was the end of your obligation to your employer. God help you if pictures from a happy hour party makes its way to Facebook, you're pretty much doomed."

Here is the good news you can control what information is visible about your personal life even if you have already posted personal content on Facebook. Eraser Max 5.0 is an affordable system of proven strategies and trade secrets designed to bury potentially embarrassing online content.

If you have potentially damaging information posted on Facebook or Twitter and would like to have removed it before it goes public then please visit http://www.removeitnow.com

Sample Article # 2 –

Jobs for Citizens Convicted of a Felony by Tyronne Jacques

Putting an End to Excessive Punishment!

Over the past month I have noticed an increase in clients requesting our help in removing old newspaper articles about a felony arrest. After about the 5th client I started to notice that they all had one thing in common; all of them had already complied with the conditions of their sentence prior to contacting me.

Many of my clients with felony convictions on their records are simply trying to get a decent job, but the felony arrest is hindering their search. To add insult to injury all of them had an old newspaper article that detailed everything that happened on the day they were arrested. The difference in between a police background check and an online line article is the article will give more details of what happen on the day of the arrest.

Newspaper reporters and law enforcement work hand in hand therefore the newspaper article is only going to reflect whatever information is released by the arresting officers. The design of a police press release is to make the suspect look like a total monster, and in many cases their acts deserve that description. But what if the suspect was acquitted of the charges, how often will the police contact the newspaper and have them update the story?

The answer is it hardly ever happens, that story of you being a monster will remain under your name in Google forever!

Now you're out looking for a job and your future employer happens to search your name in Google, yikes!

This scenario plays out every day as people who were wrongfully charge, and others who have complied with the conditions of their sentence are repeatedly punished by old online articles still appearing in search results. My clients are amongst the exceptions because many people who are convicted of a felony simply give up and result to whatever was familiar.

Here is the good news; people convicted of a felony still own the rights to their name / brand. Remove It Now.com will teach you how to control the information that is visible about your online identity. Remove It Now.com is a system of proven strategies that will help you remove negative information that is appearing under your search results.

Give yourself a fighting chance by removing that old outdated newspaper article about your past with Remove It Now.com

Sample Press Release # 1 - APEX

Apex Investment Consulting – Dominated The Australian Markets now setting their sights on the US.

Welcome to Market Domination!

Apex Investment Consulting has been enjoying an impressive run since 2005; in fact it is safe to say they have emerged from more turbulent markets than the US without a scratch.

In a recent interview with Luke MacDonald Director of the Australian based firm he says that the key to their success is creating a perfect blend of Profits and Profitability.

"The main similarity between profit and profitability is that they both can be used as a gauge for the revenue generated by a company. The main difference is that profit can only be used as a gauge for the money made in the past, but profitability can project whether or not a company will continue to make money.

To have profitability, the company must reinvest capital back into the company to keep it profitable. "

Apex Investment Consulting has diffidently shown a tremendous profit for their investors which can be credited as the reason they shatter client retention records for 2009. In just a brief interview with Luke MacDonald here is what we discovered.

For a company to be more profitable they have to be as accurate as possible with their projections, and make wise decisions as they return to their reinvestment strategies. Most business executives agree that a business should reinvest 60% of the profits back into the business. If you stop investing in your business, then business will stop investing in you.

A company can have the large profits, but another company similar in nature could have better profitability. To increase profitability a company should continue to develop new products. Another profitability strategy requires that the company make updated changes to existing products in order to attract a broader base of consumers...

At the core of Profitability is making good use of returns on investments while developing services and products that will continue to create a profit for the company, and most importantly the investors.

Things that make some companies more profitable than others is understanding what their targeted customers want, and how much they are willing to pay for it. Since gas prices are high, many consumers are switching to hybrid cars.

At this point in the history of auto sales and manufacturing it is probably wise to invest in auto manufactures who are leading the way in hybrid production.

This report on profits and profitability was only a brief lecture in how to build the perfect portfolio for your investment dollars. If you are new to the world of investments then I would strongly suggest that you partner with an experience professional before venturing out on your own.

Apex Investment -Leading Investment and Index Trading is diffidently a good place to start in deciding which markets are best for your long term strategy.

Today is as good as any to begin researching investment options. If you need assistant planning a more secure investment strategy then I suggest that you give the experts at Apex Investments services a call.

Simply visit their website at http

Sample Press Release # 2 – IMAGEMAX PR

Helping Stop Cyber Bullying - Image Max PR Sells Over 2,500 Remove It Now.com Entries in Less Than a Month

Image Max, an aggressive cyber slander defense firm, has sold over 2,500 Remove It Now.com entries that give four steps to remove negative articles from the first page of Google results. Remove It Now.com is now available for $19.95.

New Orleans, La – Premier cyber-slander defense firm, Image Max PR, recently announced it has sold more than 2,500 Remove It Now.com entries since March 30, 2010.

Remove It Now.com is a revolutionary concept that helps individuals and businesses stop and prevent <u>cyber slander</u>. For only $19.95, the online reputation management system can remove embarrassing and often false information from the first page of Google results.

The program continues to beat sales records as more and more people learn through the web and TV commercials running in selected markets the value that online reputation management offers.

Remove It Now.com gives four easy steps that users can take to quickly and effectively <u>remove negative articles</u> from search results.

Tyronne Jacques, CEO of Image Max (http://www.removeitnow.com), explains the value of the Remove It Now.com system stating, "Individuals and businesses are now to looking to Google to find out information about potential employees or the reputation of companies. With over 90% of users accepting the first page of results as factual, one complaint or bad record can affect your online reputation and your ability to get a job or close a business deal. The Remove It Now.com system will teach you how to fight Google and win."

The system has also been useful for parents to protect their children. An emerging problem on the web is cyber bullying. With the growth of online social networks a child's reputation and emotional well-being is at the whim of others who find less accountability in posting their attacks online.

Often parents do not find out if bullying is happening until it is too painful for the child. Parents can now be proactive to stop cyber bullying by getting Cyber Bully Alerts with the Remove It Now.com system which notifies them when their child's name is being posted on the web. This system provides parents with the information and tools necessary to defend their children from this terrible issue.

"If your child is not being bullied then consider yourself blessed, but also use this opportunity to find out if your child is actually bullying someone else.

Together we can help bring an end to this growing problem," notes Jacques, who is a parent of a teen himself.

Everyone should be taking proactive steps to protect their children, themselves and their businesses on the web. The large volume of sales of the Remove It Now.com program shows that more people are finding the value of this proven online reputation management system.

Tyronne Jacques is available for interviews regarding Remove It Now.com and Image Max PR. To schedule an interview contact Ron Collins, the CFO of Image Max PR.

About Image Max PR: The Louisiana-based cyber slander defense firm, Image Max PR, was founded in 2007 as part of a project to improve the negative reputation of New Orleans.

For more information please visit our website – http://www.removeitnow.com

ABOUT THE AUTHOR

Tyronne (TJ) Jacques is the founder of Remove It Now.com, an online community dedicated to protecting consumers from online slander and cyber bully attacks. He is an expert in the field of Entertainment PR and Brand Development. Tyronne Jacques is also the Executive Director of Image Max PR which specializes in Brand Development, and Online Brand Protection. In addition to his day to day responsibilities in the field of public relations, he has also published over 500 articles on Public Relations and Student Cyber Safety Topics.

Tyronne Jacques has a passion for helping small business owners restore their reputations after a vicious online attack. Because of his expertise in libel cases, he has provided expert testimony in civil cases involving Defamation of Character.

TJ is an expert in SEO (Search Engine Optimization) which is the art of increasing the search engine visibility and page ranking of websites. Tyronne Jacques currently hosts a monthly webinar on how to build a cash generating website for only $5.

Tyronne Jacques is also the Author of "Become Your Own Publicist" an online resource dedicated to educating consumers on how to fight Google and win.

TJ lives and works in his beautiful hometown of New Orleans, Louisiana and is very proud of his role in the recovery efforts during the aftermath of Hurricane Katrina.

We invite you visit his website at http://www.removeitnow.com or email him directly at tj@removeitnow.com

Made in the USA
Lexington, KY
21 December 2010